THE HIDDEN PLACES OF

NORTHUMBERLAND AND DURHAM

Northumberland, County Durham, Tyne and Wear and the Tees Valley

By Peter Long

Published by: Travel Publishing Ltd, 7a Apollo House,
Calleva Park, Aldermaston, Berks, RG7 8TN

ISBN 1-904-434-37-1

© Travel Publishing Ltd

First published 1992, second edition 1995,
third edition 1998, fourth edition 2001,
fifth edition 2003, sixth edition 2005

All advertisements in this publication have been accepted in
good faith by Travel Publishing and have not necessarily
been endorsed by the company.

All information is included by the publishers in good faith
and is believed to be correct at the time of going to press.
No responsibility can be accepted for errors.

Foreword

This is the 6th edition of the **Hidden Places of Northumberland & Durham** which has been fully updated. In this respect we would like to thank the many Tourist Information Centres in each county for helping us update the editorial content. Regular readers will note that the pages of the guide have been extensively redesigned to allow more information to be presented on the many places to visit in Norhumberland, County Durham, Tyne & Wear and the Tees Valley . In addition, although you will still find details of places of interest and advertisers of places to stay, eat and drink included under each village, town or city, these are now cross referenced to more detailed information contained in a separate, easy-to-use section of the book. This section is also available as a free supplement from the local Tourist Information Offices.

Northumberland offers the visitor plenty of picturesque places to visit such as the Kielder Forest, the Cheviot Hills, Holy Island, and the many miles of attractive coastline. Hadrian's Roman Wall also stretches across this largely unspoilt county. **County Durham** is blessed with an incredibly strong history that runs deep with industrial heritage. The landscape still shows evidence of coal mining traditions, but the spoil heaps and pit heads have now all but disappeared. The county encompasses the beautiful and historic City of Durham and, like its northern neighbour, has an impressive number of castles, churches and historic houses.

The **Hidden Places** series is a collection of easy to use local and national travel guides taking you on a relaxed but informative tour of Britain and Ireland. Our books contain a wealth of interesting information on the history, the countryside, the towns and villages and the more established places of interest. But they also promote the more secluded and little known visitor attractions and places to stay, eat and drink many of which are easy to miss unless you know exactly where you are going.

We include hotels, inns, restaurants, public houses, teashops, various types of accommodation, historic houses, museums, gardens, and many other attractions all of which are comprehensively indexed. Most places are accompanied by an attractive photograph and are easily located by using the map at the beginning of each chapter. We do not award merit marks or rankings but concentrate on describing the more interesting, unusual or unique features of each place with the aim of making the reader's stay in the local area an enjoyable and stimulating experience.

Whether you are visiting Northumberland and Durham for business or pleasure or are a local inhabitant, we do hope that you enjoy reading and using this book. We are always interested in what readers think of places covered (or not covered) in our guides so please do not hesitate to use the reader reaction forms provided to give us your considered comments. We also welcome any general comments which will help us improve the guides themselves. Finally if you are planning to visit any other corner of the British Isles we would like to refer you to the order form for other **Hidden Places** titles to be found at the rear of the book and to the Travel Publishing website at **www.travelpublishing.co.uk.**

Travel Publishing

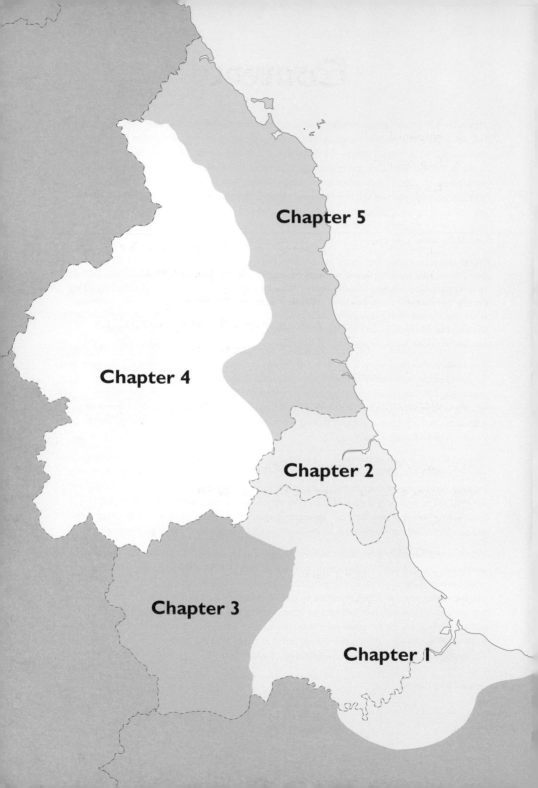

Contents

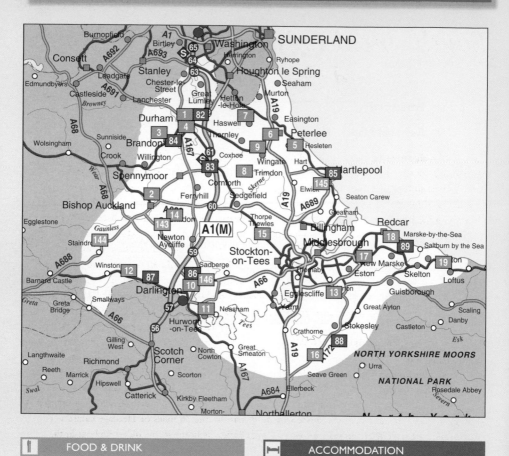

🍴 FOOD & DRINK

1	The Garden House, Durham	p 4, 98, 126
2	Tut 'n' Shive, Bishop Aukland	p 9, 98
3	Stonebridge Inn, Neville's Cross	p 5, 98
4	The Bay Horse Inn, Brandon Village	p 7, 99, 126
5	The Ship Inn, High Hesleden	p 14, 99
6	The Royal George, Old Shotton Village	p 14, 100
7	The Wayfarers Inn, Haswell	p 15, 100
8	The Red Lion, Trimdon Village	p 15, 100
9	The Fir Tree, Wingate	p 15, 100
10	The George, Darlington	p 16, 101, 127
11	The Otter & Fish, Hurworth-on-Tees	p 17, 101
12	Lord Nelson, Gainford	p 18, 101
13	Pathfinders, Maltby	p 19, 101
14	The Bay Horse , Middridge	p 17, 102
15	The Vane Arms, Thorpe Thewles	p 19, 103
16	The Sutton Arms, Faceby	p 20, 103
17	The Half Moon, Lazenby	p 20, 103
18	Zetland Hotel, Marske-by-the-Sea	p 21, 104, 127
19	Mars Inn, Loftus	p 21, 104

🛏 ACCOMMODATION

82	The Garden House, Durham	p 4, 98, 126
83	Ash House, Cornforth	p 7, 126
84	The Bay Horse Inn, Brandon Village	p 7, 99, 126
85	Altonlea Lodge, Seaton Carew	p 13, 127
86	The George, Darlington	p 16, 101, 127
87	The Bridge House, Piercebridge	p 18, 127
88	Dromonby Hall Farm, Kirkby-in-Cleveland	p 20, 127
89	Zetland Hotel, Marske-by-the-Sea	p 21, 104, 127

🏛 PLACES OF INTEREST

143	Locomotion: The National Railway Museum, Shildon	p 10, 145
144	Raby Castle, Staindrop	p 11, 146
145	Hartlepool's Maritime Experience, Hartlepool	p 12, 147
146	Darlington Railway Centre & Museum, Darlington	p 16, 147

South and Central County Durham and the Tees Valley

County Durham's prosperity was founded on coal mining, and nowhere is this more apparent than in the central and southern parts of the county. Coal has been mined here for centuries, but it wasn't until the 18th century that the industry was established on a commercial basis. When the railways arrived in the early 19th century, the industry prospered, creating great wealth for the landowners, and frequently great danger and misery for the miners. Now that the industry has all but disappeared, the scars it created are being swept away. Spoil heaps have been cleared or grassed over, pitheads demolished and old industrial sites tidied up. Colliery villages such as Pity Me, Shiney Row, Bearpark, Sunniside and Quebec still exist – tight-knit communities that retain an old-style sense of belonging and sharing, and even in the most unprepossessing of villages there are delightful surprises to be discovered, such as the near-perfect Saxon church at Escomb.

Coal may have been king, but County Durham's countryside has always supported an important farming industry, and Central and South Durham still retain a gentle landscape of fields, woodland, streams and narrow country lanes. This area stretches from the East Coast to the Pennines in the west, and from the old border with Yorkshire in the south to the edge of the Tyne and the Wear conurbations in the north. Within this area there are picturesque villages, cottages, grand houses, museums, snug pubs, old churches and castles aplenty.

The coastline too has been cleaned up. An 11-mile coastal footpath snakes through the district of Easington from Seaham Hall Beach in the north to Crimdon Park in the south. Much of it is along clifftops with spectacular views down onto the beaches. This coastal area has recently been designated as a National Nature Reserve. Parts of what were County Durham, Cleveland and North Yorkshire have been incorporated into an area now known as Tees Valley, which includes the towns of Darlington, Stockton-on-Tees, Hartlepool, Middlesbrough and Saltburn-by-the-Sea and is blessed with many reminders of a rich maritime heritage. Captain Cook was born in Middlesbrough in 1728, and his story is told in the Captain Cook Birthplace Museum in that town. In nearby Stockton is a replica of his ship HM Bark *Endeavour*. At Hartlepool lies HMS *Trincomalee*, the oldest warship afloat. Saltburn's coast is a recognised part of the 36 miles of Heritage Coast, and Redcar is home to the oldest lifeboat in the world, housed in the Zetland Lifeboat Museum.

Travelling around the region the visitor is also constantly reminded of its rich social, industrial and Christian heritage. The Romans marched along Dere Street in County Durham, and in the 9th and 10th centuries holy men carried the body of St Cuthbert with them as they sought a place of refuge from the marauding Vikings. The railways were born in the county in 1825, with the opening of the famous Stockton and Darlington Railway.

Dominating the whole area is the city of Durham - one of Europe's finest small cities. It was here, in 1832, that England's third great university was established. The towns of Darlington, Stockton-on-Tees, Hartlepool and Bishop Auckland are all worthy of exploration.

DURHAM CITY

Arriving in Durham by train, the visitor is presented with what must be one of the most breathtaking urban views in Europe. Towering over the tumbling roofs of the city are the magnificent Durham Cathedral and Castle.

The Cathedral is third only to Canterbury and York in ecclesiastical significance, but excels them in architectural splendour, and is the finest and grandest example of Norman architecture in Europe. This was the power base of the wealthy Prince Bishops of Durham who once exercised king-like powers in an area known as the Palatinate of Durham. The powers vested in them by William I permitted them to administer civil and criminal law, issue pardons, hold their own parliament, mint their own money, create baronetcies, and give market charters. They could even raise their own army. Though these powers were never exercised in later years, they continued in theory right up until 1836, when the last of the Prince Bishops, Bishop William Van Mildert, died. The Palatinate Courts, however, were only abolished in 1971. It is little wonder that the County Council now proudly presents the county to visitors as 'the Land of the Prince Bishops'.

The Cathedral owes its origin to the monks of Lindisfarne, who, in AD 875, fled from Viking attacks, taking with them the coffin of St Cuthbert, shepherd saint of Northumbria. In AD 883 they settled at Chester-le-Street. However, further Viking raids in AD 980 caused them to move once more, and they eventually arrived at a more easily defended site about ten miles to the south, where the River Wear makes a wide loop round a rocky outcrop. Here, in Durham, they built the 'White Church', where St Cuthbert's remains were finally laid to rest.

The present building was begun by William de St Carileph or St Calais, Bishop of Durham from 1081 to 1096. William arrived at the White Church, bringing with him holy relics and a group of monks and scholars from Monkwearmouth and Jarrow. Forced to flee to Normandy in

View over Durham City

1088, having been accused of plotting against William Rufus, William returned in 1091 after a pardon, determined to replace the little church with a building of the size and style of the splendid new churches he saw being built in France at that time. In August 1093 the foundation stones were laid, witnessed by King Malcolm III of Scotland, famed as the soldier who slew Macbeth in battle.

The main part of the great building was erected in a mere 40 years, but over ensuing centuries each generation has added magnificent work and detail of its own, such as the 14th century Episcopal Throne, said to be the highest in Christendom, and the Neville Screen made from creamy marble. On the North Door is a replica of the 12th century Sanctuary knocker used by fugitives seeking a haven. They were allowed to remain within the church for 37 days, after which time, if they had failed to settle their affairs, they were given a safe passage to the coast carrying a cross and wearing a distinctive costume.

Nothing is more moving, however, than the simple fragments of carved wood which survive from St Cuthbert's coffin, made for the saint's body in AD 698 and carried around the North of England by his devoted followers before being laid to rest in the mighty Cathedral. The fragments are now kept in the **Treasures of St Cuthbert Exhibition**, within the Cathedral, with examples of the Prince

Bishops' own silver coins. In recognition of the renewed interest in the life of St Cuthbert, the Cathedral is now officially called the Cathedral Church of Christ, the Blessed Mary the Virgin and St Cuthbert of Durham. **Sacred Journey**, at the Gala Theatre in Millennium Place, is a spectacular Giant Screen tourist attraction telling the story of the city and the life and death of St Cuthbert.

Durham Castle, sharing the same rocky peninsula and standing close to the cathedral, was founded in 1072 and belonged to the Prince Bishops. Such was the impregnability of the site that Durham was one of the few towns in Northumbria that was never captured by the Scots. Among the motte-and-bailey castle's most impressive features are the Chapel, dating from 1080, and the Great Hall, which was built in the middle of the 13th century. The 18th

3   STONEBRIDGE INN

Stonebridge, Neville's Cross, western outskirts of Durham

Cooking, value for money and service all excel at the **Stonebridge Inn** on the western edge of the city.

see page 98

•

Durham Cathedral contains the tomb of the Venerable Bede (AD 673-735), saint, scholar-monk and Britain's first and pre-eminent historian. Bede spent most of his life teaching at Jarrow and was originally buried there. His body found its final resting place in the galilee of the Cathedral in 1370.

•

Durham Cathedral

On the western outskirts of the city of Durham, and straddling the A167, is the site of the Battle of Neville's Cross, fought in 1346 between Scotland and England. The Scottish army was heavily defeated, and the Scottish king, David II, was taken prisoner.

century gatehouse has a Norman core, as does the massive keep, which was rebuilt in Victorian times.

Only open to the public at limited times (Tel: 0191 334 4106), the Castle is now used as a hall of residence for the students of Durham University, and The Great Hall serves as the Dining Hall of University College. But students and visitors should beware - the castle is reputedly haunted by no less than three ghosts. One is said to be of Jane, wife of Bishop Van Mildert, and takes the form of the top half of a woman in 19th-century dress. She glides along the

Norman Gallery, leaving the scent of apple blossom in her wake. A second spirit is of university tutor Frederick Copeman, who, in 1880, threw himself off the tower of the Cathedral. His ghost is said to haunt his former room off the Norman Gallery. A further apparition, who has been seen at various locations within the castle, is a cowled monk.

The university, England's third oldest after Oxford and Cambridge - was founded in 1832 by Bishop Van Mildert. In 1837 it moved into Durham Castle, though today its many buildings are scattered throughout the south of the city. The importance of the whole area surrounding the Cathedral and Castle was recognised in 1987, when it was designated a UNESCO World Heritage Site.

A favourite walk past the site starts at Framwellgate Bridge or Elvet Bridge and follows the footpaths that run through the woodlands on each bank of the River Wear, around the great loop. The path along the inside of the loop goes past The Old Fulling Mill, situated below the Cathedral, which now houses the **University of Durham Museum of Archaeology** containing material from excavations in and around the city. Prebends Bridge offers spectacular views of the Cathedral. If walking isn't to your taste you can take a cruise along the river from Elvet Bridge.

The rest of Durham reflects the long history of the Castle and Cathedral it served. There are

Morris Dancers in Market Square, Durham

winding streets, such as Saddler Street and Silver Street (whose names attest to their medieval origin), the ancient Market Place, elegant Georgian houses - particularly around South Bailey, and quiet courtyards and alleyways. Much of Durham's shopping area is closed to traffic, making for a more relaxed atmosphere. There are several churches worth visiting, including St Nicholas's Church in the Market Place, St Mary le Bow Church in North Bailey, which houses the **Durham Heritage Centre and Museum**, and St Oswald's Church in Church Street. Their presence highlights the fact that in medieval times this was a great place of pilgrimage.

The **Durham Light Infantry Museum and Durham Art Gallery** at Aykley Heads tells the story of the county's own regiment, which was founded in 1758 and lasted right up until 1968. The horrors of the First World War are shown, as is a reconstruction of a Durham street during the Second World War. Individual acts of bravery are also remembered, such as the story of Adam Wakenshaw, the youngest of a family of 13, who refused to leave his comrades after his arm was blown off. He died in action, and was awarded a Victoria Cross. The art gallery has a changing exhibition of paintings and sculpture.

The **Durham University Oriental Museum** houses a collection of Oriental art of great importance, with exhibits from ancient Egypt, Tibet, India, China, Persia and Japan. Located in parkland off Elvet Hill Road to the south of the city, the museum entrance is guarded by two stately Chinese lion-dogs.

The university also runs the 18-acre **Botanical Garden**, on Hollingside Lane (off the A167) on the south side of the city. The gardens include a large collection of North American trees, including junior-sized giant redwoods, a series of small 'gardens-within-gardens' and walks through mature woodland. Two display greenhouses with trees and plants from all over the world feature cacti and a tropical 'jungle'.

Crook Hall and its Gardens in Frankland Lane, close to the River Wear, offer many delights, including the Secret Walled Gardens, the Shakespeare Gardens, the Cathedral Garden and the Silver & White Garden, an orchard and a maze. The medieval manor house has a Jacobean Room haunted by the White Lady. Call 0191 384 8028 for opening times.

AROUND DURHAM CITY

BRANCEPETH

4 miles SW of Durham on the A690

Brancepeth is a small estate village built by Matthew Russell in the early 19th century, with picturesque Georgian cottages and an 18th century rectory. To the south, in parkland, is the imposing Brancepeth Castle. The original 13th century castle was owned by the Nevills, Earls of Westmorland,

4/84 THE BAY HORSE INN

Brandon Village, SW of Durham

The **Bay Horse Inn** is a fine tourist base with 10 chalet-style bedrooms and a very good restaurant.

see pages 99, 126

83   ASH HOUSE

Cornforth, nr Durham

Period charm and modern amenities combine at **Ash House**, an early Victorian house in a quiet, attractive setting

see page 126

Main Street, Brancepeth

A place definitely worth visiting near Lanchester is Hall Hill Farm, on the B6296 four miles south west of the village. It's a real working farm, open to the public all year round.

and was for many years the headquarters of the Durham Light Infantry.

Close to the castle are the remains of St Brandon's Church. In 1998 a fire destroyed everything but the four walls and tower of what was once a beautiful and historic building. The church's magnificent woodwork, commissioned by its rector John Cosin in the early 17th century, was completely destroyed. Cosin went on to become Bishop of Durham, and restored many churches in the county. Thanks to an appeal, work is under way to restore the church.

FINCHALE PRIORY

4 miles N of Durham off the A167

On a minor road off the A167 lies 13th century Finchale (pronounced Finkle) Priory. It was built by the monks of Durham Cathedral as a holiday retreat on the site of a hermitage founded by St Godric in about 1115. The ruins sit on a loop of the Wear in a beautiful location, across the river from Cocken Wood Picnic Area, which is linked to the Priory by a bridge.

LANCHESTER

8 miles NW of Durham on the A691

Lanchester owes its name to the Roman fort of Longovicium ('The Long Fort'), which stood on a hilltop half a mile to the southwest. The fort was built to guard Dere Street, the Roman road that linked York and the north. The scant remains sit on private land, however, and can't be visited. Stone

Finchale Priory

from the fort was used in the mostly-Norman All Saints Church, and Roman pillars can be seen supporting the north aisle. There is also a Roman altar in the south porch and some superb 12th century carvings over the vestry door in the chancel.

The area to the south of Lanchester was a typical County Durham mining area, with several small colliery villages such as Quebec, Esh Winning, Tow Law and Cornsay Colliery.

PITTINGTON

3 miles E of Durham off the B1283

A small village, Pittington contains one of County Durham's hidden gems - the Saxon-Norman St Laurence's Church at Hallgarth. The present church dates from the 11th century, on the site of what is believed to be an even earlier Saxon church. The 12th century paintings of St Cuthbert are well worth seeing.

BISHOP AUCKLAND

Bishop Auckland is an ancient town, standing on what was Dere Street - an old Roman road. Like many County Durham towns, it owed its later prosperity to coal mining. When the surrounding pits closed, the town went into decline, but it is now gradually rediscovering itself as new industries are established. As its name implies, this was part of the territory of the Prince Bishops of Durham, who controlled what was

then a scattering of small villages. Rapid expansion occurred during the 19th century and Bishop Auckland became an important market town and administrative centre for the region.

Auckland Castle, at one time the principal country residence of the Prince Bishops, is now the official residence of the Bishop of Durham. The castle began as a small 12th century manor house

Gothic Gateway to Auckland Castle

---

2   TUT 'N' SHIVE

Newgate Street, Bishop Auckland

The **Tut 'n' Shive** is a cheerful local serving well-kept real ales and good-value lunches.

see *page 98*

On display in a working men's club at West Auckland can be found the most unlikely of trophies - the World Cup, no less. In 1910 the village's football team headed off to Italy to represent England in the first ever 'World Cup'. The team competed against teams from Germany, Italy and Switzerland, and remarkably won the cup when it beat Juventus 2-0 in the final. The team returned the following year to defend its title, and again won the trophy, which earned them the right to retain it for all time. Sadly the trophy seen today is actually a replica, as the original was stolen.

143 LOCOMOTION: THE NATIONAL RAILWAY MUSEUM

Shildon

A fascinating insight into the early days of rail and steam power, including many original exhibits.

 see page 145

and over the years successive bishops have added to it; looking at it today, it appears largely 17th or 18th century. But the fabric is still basically medieval, although parts of it were destroyed during the Civil War, when it was the headquarters of Sir Arthur Hazlerigg, Governor of the North. Bishop Cosin set about making it windproof and watertight after the Restoration, turning the Great Hall into a magnificent private chapel in 1665. Dedicated to St Peter, it is reputed to be the largest private chapel in Europe. Tel: 01388 601627.

A market has been held in Bishop Auckland for centuries. Opposite the present market place is the imposing Franco-Flemish Bishop Auckland Town Hall, built in the early 1860s.

While the villages immediately surrounding Bishop Auckland are mainly industrial, there are still some attractions worth seeing. At South Church is the cathedralesque St Andrew's Church, 157 feet long and said to be the largest parish church in the county.

AROUND BISHOP AUCKLAND

BINCHESTER

1 mile N of Bishop Auckland off the A689

Binchester Roman Fort, known to the Romans as Vinovia, was built in around AD 80. It was one of a chain of forts built along Dere Street, and has the best preserved Roman military bathhouse in Britain, complete with a pillared hypocaust

heating system. In addition to acting as a military centre controlling the local area, the fort also provided a stopping-off place for troops and supplies heading towards Hadrian's Wall. A portion of Dere Street has been preserved here.

CROOK

5 miles NW of Bishop Auckland on the A689

Crook is a small, spacious, town with a wide square, which, in summer, is full of flowers. At one time it was a centre of coal mining, and the quaintly named Billy Row to the north of the town centre is a typical coalfield hamlet of miners' cottages.

ESCOMB

2 miles NW of Bishop Auckland off the A688

In the small village of Escomb is one of the true hidden gems of County Durham – the 7th century Church of St John the Evangelist church, built using stone from nearby Binchester Roman Fort. This is one of only three complete Saxon churches in Britain, and is typically Saxon in layout, with its long, high nave and tiny chancel arch. In the south wall of the nave is a curious sundial surrounded by serpents and surmounted by what may be a mythical beast. This church is one of Northern Europe's finest examples of early Christian architecture.

SHILDON

2 miles SE of Bishop Auckland on the B6282

Timothy Hackworth served from 1825 as the resident engineer on the Stockton to Darlington

Railway. In 1840 he resigned and left in order to develop the Soho Engine Works at Shildon, and make his own locomotives. The first trains to run in Russia and Nova Scotia were built here. Today the Engine Works, plus his house, form **Locomotion: The National Railway Museum**. The displays, including 60 vehicles and a workshop, give a fascinating insight into the early days of rail and steam power in England. Among the main attractions is a full-size replica of the *Sans Pareil* locomotive, built by Hackworth in 1829 for the Rainhill Trials on the Liverpool to Manchester railways. Tel: 01388 772000

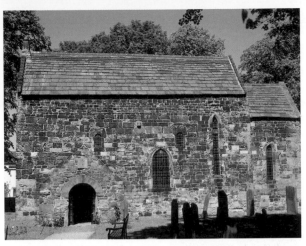

Saxon Church, Escomb

STAINDROP

7 miles SW of Bishop Auckland on the A688

Set in a magnificent 200-acre deer park on the outskirts of the village, **Raby Castle** is one of the country's finest medieval castles - a romantic, fairy-tale building, which was once the home of the powerful Nevill family. Built in the 14th century, it houses a fine art collection and sumptuous interiors. In the 16th century over 700 barons assembled in the great Baron's Hall to plot the overthrow of Elizabeth 1 – an action which was to cost the Nevill family dearly, for it resulted in the castle and all the Nevill estates being seized by the Crown. In 1626 the castle was leased to Sir Henry Vane, James 1's Secretary of State, and has remained with the Vane family ever since. The castle was besieged during the Civil War, but luckily survived and remains an impressive example of defensive and domestic architecture. Much of the interior is now Georgian and Victorian, although the Great Kitchen remains virtually unaltered

Village Green, Staindrop

144 RABY CASTLE

Staindrop

Dating back in parts to the 14th century, Raby Castle gives an insight into life throughout the ages.

🏛 *see page 146*

11

145 HARTLEPOOL'S MARITIME EXPERIENCE

Hartlepool

One of the top Heritage and History attractions in the UK featuring a re-creation of an 18th century sea port.

 see page 147

since its construction over 600 years ago. The Castle, the beautiful walled garden and the coach house are all open to the public. Tel: 01833 660202

Staindrop itself is a delightful, very typical, Durham village with a long village green lined with Georgian houses. St Mary's Church, with its Saxon core, houses tombs of the Nevill and Vane families.

WITTON-LE-WEAR

4 miles NW of Bishop Auckland off the A68

Overlooking the River Wear are the hillside terraces of the village of Witton-le-Wear, noted for its handsome green, its open views, attractive cottages and a pele tower attached to fragments of a medieval manor house in the High Street. **Low Barns Nature Reserve** is a 40-hectare reserve with a nature trail, bird hides, observatory, woodland, ponds, meadow, lakes and river. The Nature Reserve and Visitor Centre are in the care of the Durham Wildlife Trust.

HARTLEPOOL

There are really two Hartlepools - the old town on the headland, and the newer part with the marina and town centre, formerly known as West Hartlepool. A proud maritime town, the old part of Hartlepool dates back centuries. In the Middle Ages it was the only port within County Durham that was allowed to trade outside the Palatinate, thus confirming its importance. After the Norman Conquest, the Bruce family, whose most notable member was Robert the Bruce, King of Scotland, acquired the town. In 1201 King John bestowed the market charter on Hartlepool and ordered that the walls be built to defend it against the marauding Scots. Today parts of the wall remain and continue to stand guard over the Headland. There is a particularly fine gatehouse, called the Sandwellgate, with solid turrets on either side. Go through the pointed archway, and you find yourself on the beach.

Built by the Bruces as a burial place, the ornate 13th century St Hilda's Church stands on the site of a monastery founded by St Aidan in AD 647. The church is dedicated to St Hilda – its most famous abbess, celebrated for her teachings and her mentoring of a poor cowherd Caedmon, now regarded as the creator of religious verse. Hilda subsequently went on to found the great monastery at Whitby, where the Synod of Whitby was held in AD 664. The church houses a collection of

Hartlepool Marina

12

religious artefacts, Saxon wall carvings and a tomb, made of Frosterley marble, believed to be that of Robert the Bruce. Parts of the cemetery were excavated in the 19th century, and some of the finds are on display in Durham and Newcastle

Hartlepool's harbour gradually went into decline, and by the early 18th century the place was no more than a fishing village. In 1835 work started on opening up the harbour once more, and rail links were established with the coalfields. But it faced stiff competition. In 1847 work started on the West Harbour and Coal Dock, and by 1860 it was thriving with timber and shipyards. Other docks were opened and Ralph Ward Jackson, a local entrepreneur, instigated the building of a new town with streets of terraced houses to house the workers. A park with many sporting and leisure facilities named in his honour is linked by a walkway to Burn Valley Gardens, the town's central green belt.

On December 16, 1914 Hartlepool was the first town in Britain to suffer from enemy action during the First World War when it was shelled from German warships lying off the coast.

Nowadays the town is a thriving shopping centre, with some interesting tourist attractions, including the Hartlepool Historic Quay and Museum. A small seaport has been constructed around one of the old docks, showing what life was like in the early part of the 19th century, when Britain was at

war with France. Grouped round the small dock are various businesses and shops, such as a printer, gunsmith, naval tailor, swordsmith and instrument maker. Visitors can also go aboard HMS *Trincomalee*, a British warship originally launched in 1817.

Next door is the **Museum of Hartlepool**, with exhibits depicting life in the town through the ages. It features tales of sea monsters and the legend of the Hartlepool

85 ALTONLEA LODGE

Seaton Carew, Hartlepool

The warmest of welcomes awaits guests at the family-run **Altonlea Lodge** near the seafront.

⊨ see page 127

Abbey Church of St Hilda, Hartlepool

5   THE SHIP INN

High Hesleden, nr Hartlepool

Lovers of good food and real ales set course from all over the region for **The Ship Inn**.

🍴 see page 99

•

In August Billingham hosts a week long Billingham International Folklore Festival. *The purpose-built Billingham Art Gallery stages exhibitions of local, national and international arts, crafts and workshops throughout the year.*

•

6   THE ROYAL GEORGE

Old Shotton Village, S of Peterlee

The **Royal George** is a popular pub serving draught ales and ciders and well-priced food.

🍴 see page 100

14

monkey. Washed ashore on a piece of wreckage during the Napoleonic Wars, local fishermen, unable to understand the monkey's gibberings, presumed it to be a French spy and hanged it from a gibbet on Fish Sands. Visitors to the museum can have coffee aboard the PSS *Wingfield Castle*, an old paddle steamer.

Close by is Jackson's Landing, a new shopping mall situated at the centre of Hartlepool's Marina. Hartlepool Art Gallery is housed within a beautifully restored Victorian church on Church Square. It features a collection of contemporary art and photographic exhibitions. A 100-feet viewing tower affords the visitor great views of the town. The local tourist information office is here too.

AROUND HARTLEPOOL

BILLINGHAM

5 miles SW of Hartlepool, off the A19

Modern Billingham grew up as a result of the great chemical plants that surrounded the River Tees. Although the town looks modern, it is in fact an ancient place, possibly founded by Bishop Ecgred of Lindisfarne in the 9th century. **St Cuthbert's Church** has a 10th century Saxon tower, and Saxon walls survive in the nave. The chancel was rebuilt and widened in 1939 to provide for the town's growing population due to the influx of workers to the chemical plants. **Billingham Beck Valley Country Park** is a country park

with wetlands, wildflower meadows and a 10-acre ecology park with a visitor centre.

ELWICK

4 miles W of Hartlepool off the A19

Elwick is a small, pretty village with patches of village green running up each side of a main street lined with neat, unassuming cottages. St Peter's Church has a nave dating from the 13th century. The chancel was rebuilt in the 17th century using materials from the previous chancel, and its tower was added on in 1813. On either side of the chancel arch are two small Saxon carvings - possibly fragments of grave markers.

HART

2 miles NW of Hartlepool on the A179

In this quiet village stands the mother church of Hartlepool – St Mary Magdalene's Church with its varied examples of architecture. The nave is Saxon, the tower and font are Norman, and the chancel is early 19th century.

On the outer wall of the White Hart Inn is a figurehead, said to have been a relic from the *Rising Sun*, which was shipwrecked off Hartlepool in 1861.

PETERLEE

6 miles N of Hartlepool off the A19

Peterlee is a new town, established in 1948 to rehouse the mining families from the colliery villages around Easington and Shotton. The town has a modern shopping centre, a tourist information office and a market. Close by is the village of

Easington, whose fine old St Mary's Church sits on a low hill. The church tower is Norman, and the interior contains some examples of Cosin-style woodwork.

Castle Eden Dene National Nature Reserve, on the south side of the town, is of national importance, being one of the largest woodlands in the North East that has not been planted or extensively altered by man. It covers 500 acres and lies in a steep-sided gorge on magnesian limestone, with a wide variety of native trees and shrubs, wild flowers, bird life and butterflies, including the Castle Eden Argus, which is found only in eastern County Durham. There is a network of footpaths, some steep and narrow. Visitors are requested to keep to paths at all times to avoid damage. Tel: 0191 586 0004

SEAL SANDS

3 miles S of Hartlepool off the A689

Standing in the shadows of Hartlepool Nuclear Power Station is Seal Sands and the Teesmouth Field Centre. Local organisations have come together to protect and enhance the marshes, tidal flats and dunes here on the north shore of the Tees estuary. The area is protected as a Nature Reserve and popular with people who come to view its large Common and Grey seal population and thousands of migratory birds.

TRIMDON

9 miles W of Hartlepool on the B1278

There are a trio of villages with the word Trimdon in their name - Trimdon Grange, Trimdon Colliery and Trimdon itself. It's a quiet village with a wide main street and the unpretentious medieval St Mary Magdalene's Church.

At Trimdon Colliery, two miles to the northeast, a great underground explosion in 1882 claimed the lives of 74 miners.

DARLINGTON

Darlington is an important regional centre serving the southern part of County Durham, Teesdale, the Tees valley and much of North Yorkshire. It was founded in Saxon times, and has a bustling town centre with one of the largest market places in England. On its west side are the Old Town Hall and indoor market, with an imposing Clock Tower designed by Alfred Waterhouse in 1864.

There are many fine buildings in Darlington, most notably St Cuthbert's Church on the east side of the market place, with its distinctive tall spire. It is almost cathedral-like in its proportions, and was built by Bishop Pudsey between 1183 and 1230 as a collegiate church. Its slender lancet windows and steep roof enhance its beauty, which has earned it the name 'The Lady of the North'.

Perhaps Darlington's greatest claim to fame lies in the role it played, with neighbouring Stockton, in the creation of the world's first commercially successful public railway, which opened in 1825. It was the Darlington Quaker and

7 THE WAYFARERS INN

Haswell, W of Easington

The **Wayfarers Inn** is a convivial pub serving a wide range of classic English dishes.

❦ *see page 100*

9 THE FIR TREE

Wingate, SE of Durham

Hospitality is in generous supply at the **Fir Tree**, which is also a great place for a meal.

❦ *see page 100*

8 THE RED LION

Trimdon Village, N of Sedgefield

An imaginative menu of home-cooked dishes keeps the customers happy at the **Red Lion**, an immaculate pub.

❦ *see page 100*

15

Market Square, Darlington

Road Station. Today it serves as the **Darlington Railway Centre and Museum** – a museum of national importance which houses relics of the pioneering Stockton and Darlington Railway. These include a replica of Stephenson's *Locomotion No 1*, a Stockton and Darlington first-class carriage built in 1846, a World War 11 newsstand, the *Derwent*, (the earliest surviving Darlington-built locomotive) and even Victorian loos. The present Darlington Station, Bank Top, was constructed at a later date as part of the East Coast line linking England with Scotland.

So much early railway history is to be seen hereabouts that British Rail have named their local Bishop Auckland-Darlington-Middlesbrough line the Heritage Line.

Continuing with the railway theme, there's an unusual engine to be seen in Morton Park – *Train* is a life-size brick sculpture, designed by sculptor David Mach. During the summer months you can see a floral replica of George Stephenson's *Locomotion No 1* in the town centre, at the foot of Post House Wynd.

10/86 THE GEORGE

Bondgate, Darlington

Real ales and good honest lunchtime food brings the locals and visitors to the **George**, which also has 4 rooms for B&B.

 see pages *101, 127*

146 DARLINGTON RAILWAY CENTRE & MUSEUM

Darlington

A superb collection of engines, carriages and wagons including Stephenson's Locomotion.

🏛 see page *147*

banker Edward Pease who became the main driving force behind the scheme to link the Durham coalfields with the port of Stockton.

The original Darlington Station, built in 1842, was located at North

Brick Sculpture, Morton Park

AROUND DARLINGTON

GAINFORD

7 miles W of Darlington on the A67

Gainford village sits just north of the Tees. At its core is a jostling collection of quaint 18th and 19th century cottages and houses grouped around a village green. At the south west corner of the green is St Mary's Church - a large church, built mostly in the 12th century from stone that is believed to have come from Piercebridge Roman fort, three miles to the east. Certainly a Roman altar was found built into the tower during the restoration of 1864-65, and it can be seen in the museum of Durham Cathedral.

Gainford Hall is a large Jacobean mansion built by the Reverend John Cradock in the early 1600s. Though not open to the public, it can be viewed from the road. It's hard to believe that in the 19th century the now quiet village of Gainford was a spa, visited by people from all over the North of England. Some way away along the banks of the Tees to the west, a basin can be seen where the sulphurous waters were collected.

HEIGHINGTON

5 miles N of Darlington off the A6072

Heighington is an attractive village with neat cottages and a large green. St Michael's Church is predominantly Norman, and has a pre-Reformation oak pulpit with prayers inscribed on it for its donors, Alexander and Agnes Fletcher. About three miles west of the village, near Bolam, is the shaft of a 9th century cross known as the Leggs Cross.

LOW DINSDALE

4 miles SE of Darlington off the A67

A visit on foot or by car to Low Dinsdale is well worth while, as the 12th century red sandstone St John the Baptist Church surrounded by copper beeches is worthy of a postcard. Opposite stands a 16th century manor house built on the site of a moated Norman manor owned by the Siward family. They later changed their name to Surtees, and became well known throughout the north.

MIDDLETON ST GEORGE

3 miles E of Darlington off the A67

Middleton St George is a pleasant village on the banks of the River Tees to the east of Darlington, close to Teesside International Airport - once an airfield from which British and Canadian bombers flew during World War II. St George's Church dates from the 13th century with 18th and 19th century additions, and stands away from the village among fields. Curiously, the stonework has been heavily patched with brick at some point. It is thought to have been built on the site of an old Saxon church and the Victorian pews are rather incongruous - rather more like old-fashioned waiting room seats than pews.

11 THE OTTER & FISH

Hurworth-on-Tees, nr Darlington

The **Otter & Fish** is a popular eating and drinking pub in a village on the River Tees.

see page 101

14 THE BAY HORSE

Middridge, S of Bishop Auckland, N of Darlington

An 18th century inn with a newly completed restaurant serving a superb menu.

see page 102

Close to Middleton St George, the village of Middleton One Row is aptly named - consisting of a single row of Georgian cottages. The cottages were inevitably altered over the years as the arrival of the railway inspired development in the region.

12 LORD NELSON

Gainford, nr Darlington

Drivers on the A67 keep an eye open for the **Lord Nelson**, a convivial village pub serving traditional English food.

🍴 see page 101

87 THE BRIDGE HOUSE

Piercebridge, nr Darlington

The Bridge House is a charming cottage-style house with 3 B&B rooms and a garden running down to the Tees.

🛏 see page 127

PIERCEBRIDGE

4½ miles W of Darlington on the A67

Driving past the picturesque village green of Piercebridge, most motorists will be unaware that they are passing through the centre of a once important Roman Fort. Piercebridge was one of a chain of forts on Dere Street, which linked the northern Roman headquarters at York with the north. Other forts in the chain were located at Catterick to the south and Binchester, just outside Bishop Auckland, to the north. The remains of the fort, which are still visible today, can be dated from coin evidence to around AD 270. The site is always open and admission is free. Finds from this site are housed in the Bowes Museum at Barnard Castle.

SEDGEFIELD

9 miles NE of Darlington on the A689

Sedgefield, well known for its National Hunt racecourse, is a small town whose market charter was issued in 1315. The grand 15th century tower of St Edmund's Church dominates the village green and the cluster of Georgian and early Victorian houses. It is famous for its intricately carved Cosin woodwork, which was on a par with the woodwork lost when Brancepeth church was destroyed by fire in 1998. Cosin's son-in-law, Denis Granville, was rector here in the late 17th century, and it was at this time that the woodwork was installed.

Hardwick Hall Country Park lies to the west of the town, beyond the A 177. Developed as a pleasure garden between 1748 and 1792 the gardens were all laid out and the ornamental buildings were designed by the architect James Paine. The hall is now a luxury hotel, but the 50-acre park with its network of woodland walks and Gothic folly is open to the public.

STOCKTON-ON-TEES

9 miles E of Darlington on the A166

Stockton-on-Tees found fame with the opening of the Stockton to Darlington railway in 1825, constructed so that coal from the mines of South Durham could have access to the Tees, where it would be shipped south to London. The opening of the railways encouraged the growth of industry, and the subsequent discovery of ironstone in the Cleveland Hills in the 1850s was to transform the fortunes of the town, providing considerable wealth for many of its citizens.

Sedgefield

In the centre of Stockton's High Street are the Old Town Hall and market cross dating from the mid 18th century, and in Theatre Yard off the High Street is the **Green Dragon Museum**, set in a former sweet factory warehouse. This lively museum features displays of local history and an excellent photographic gallery.

The redbrick parish church was completed in 1713 and is one of only a handful of Anglican churches in England without a dedication. Its official title is The Parish Church of Stockton-on-Tees, though for many years it has been informally called St Thomas's. This unofficial dedication came from a chapel of ease that stood on the site when Stockton was a part of the parish of Norton.

Captain James Cook is said to have served the early part of his apprenticeship in Stockton. A full-size replica of his ship, HM Bark *Endeavour* is moored at Castlegate Quay on Stockton's riverside. Alongside is the *Teesside Princess*, a river cruiser that takes visitors on a pleasure trip as far inland as Yarm, stopping at Preston Hall.

Other famous characters include John Walker, the inventor of the humble friction match, who was born in Stockton in 1781, and Thomas Sheraton, the furniture maker and designer, born here in 1751 and married in St Mary's Church, Norton. One of the town's citizens with a more unusual claim to fame was Ivy Close, who won Britain's first ever beauty contest in 1908.

Preston Hall Museum, set in 110 acres of parkland to the south of the town on the banks of the Tees, is housed in the former home of the local shipbuilder Robert Ropner. Exhibits describe how life was lived in the area at the time the Hall was built in 1825. There is a re-created period street, a fully furnished drawing room of the 1820s and a collection of arms and armoury in the cellar. The museum's most famous exhibit is *The Diceplayers*, painted by Georges de la Tour in the 17th century.

Stockton may no longer be a busy port, but in recent years there has been a lot of development

13 PATHFINDERS

Maltby, nr Stockton-on-Tees

Traditional cooking and well-kept ales are major attractions at **Pathfinders**, a charming village pub with a strong local following.

see page 101

15 THE VANE ARMS

Thorpe Thewles, Stockton-on-Tees

Motorists on the road between Sedgefield and Stockton take a break at the **Vane Arms** to enjoy super home cooking.

see page 103

High Street, Stockton-on-Tees

88 DROMONBY HALL FARM

Kirkby-in-Cleveland, nr Stokesley

Dromonby Hall Farm combines comfortable B&B accommodation with lovely country views.

see page 127

---

17 THE HALF MOON

Lazenby, E of Middlesbrough

The **Half Moon** is a well-run, traditional pub serving real ales, snacks and meals throughout the day. No smoking.

see page 103

---

 16 THE SUTTON ARMS

Faceby, S of Middlesbrough

The **Sutton Arms** is an immaculate village inn with an excellent reputation for food and drink.

see page 103

---

along the banks of the Tees. The spectacular £54 million Tees Barrage, built to stop the flow of pollution from the chemical plants being carried upstream by the tides, has transformed an 11-mile stretch of river. Features include Britain's finest purpose-built White Water canoe slalom course, navigation lock, fish pass and recreation site with picnic area.

AROUND STOCKTON

YARM

4 miles S of Stockton on the A67

Set within a loop of the River Tees, Yarm was a prosperous river port as far back as the 14th century. Its broad main street, one of the widest in England, is lined with some fine Georgian houses and coaching inns, but the bustling river traffic has gone. Standing in the centre of this elegant street is the Town Hall of 1710 with marks on its walls recording the levels of past river floods, but the town's most impressive structure is the railway viaduct with its 40 arches soaring above the rooftops and extending for almost half a mile. It was at a meeting in Yarm's George & Dragon Hotel in 1820 that plans were drawn up for the Stockton & Darlington Railway, the first of all passenger-carrying railways.

MIDDLESBROUGH

Dominating the skyline of this busy town is the **Transporter Bridge**, opened in 1911 and the only working bridge of its kind in England. The bridge can carry nine cars or 200 people on each crossing. Captain Cook was born in Middlesbrough in 1728, and in the **Captain Cook Birthplace Museum** in Stewart Park, Marton, visitors can chart his life story and experience life below decks in the 18th century through original objects and hands-on displays. Tel: 01642 311211. Also well worth a visit when in Middlesbrough is the Dorman Museum, with themed displays of natural history, social history and world cultures.

On the southeastern edge of Middlesbrough is the National Trust's **Ormesby Hall**, a beautiful 18th century mansion with a magnificent stable block attributed to Carr of York and a superb model railway layout and exhibition. Tel: 01642 324188

AROUND MIDDLESBROUGH

KIRKLEATHAM

5 miles E of Middlesbrough on the A174

Two good reasons for a visit here. **Kirkleatham Museum** is a 17th century house with exhibitions on art, coast and country, and the region's ironstone mining and iron and steel heritage, with activities for children and family groups. Tel: 01642 479500. **Kirkleatham Owl Centre** has one of the country's most important collections of owls, also falcons, buzzards, vultures, kites and caracaras. Call 01642 480512 for opening times.

GUISBOROUGH

8 miles E of Middlesbrough on the A171

The stark ruins of **Guisborough Priory** stand on an elevated site overlooked by the Cleveland Hills. Founded by the great landowner Robert de Bruis II in 1119, the monastery became one of the most powerful in Yorkshire. Much extended in 1200, and rebuilt after a fire destroyed the whole site, the estate was sold in 1540 to a Thomas Chaloner, who cannibalised much of the fabric to grace ornamental gardens at his grand mansion nearby. Nothing remains of that mansion, and of the Priory itself the great arch at the east end is the most striking survival. The grounds are a popular venue for picnics.

Guisborough

REDCAR

This popular town and resort on the coast is home to the oldest lifeboat in the world, on display at the **Zetland Lifeboat Museum**. It was built in 1802 by H Greathead and stands among exhibitions on fishing history, models, photographs, paintings and cards in a handsome listed building in King Street. Tel: 01642 494311

AROUND REDCAR

SALTBURN-BY-THE-SEA

5 miles SE of Redcar on the A174

This charming seaside town (complete with a pier) at the northern end of the 36-mile Heritage Coast is largely the work of the Victorians. It stands on a cliff high above a long, sandy beach, and to transport visitors from the town to the promenade and beach the ingenious water-balanced **Inclined Tramway** was built. It is still in use, the oldest such tramway to have survived in Britain. A miniature (15" gauge) railway runs from the seafront to the **Valley Gardens** and the **Woodland Centre**, set between the formal pleasure gardens and the wild natural woodland beyond. The pre-Victorian Saltburn was a notorious haunt of smugglers, and those days are brought to life in the **Saltburn Smugglers Heritage Centre**, set in old fishermen's cottages next to the Ship Inn in Old Saltburn. Tel: 01287 625252

18/89 ZETLAND HOTEL

Marske-by-the-Sea, below Redcar

The **Zetland** is a handsome hotel with six guest bedrooms, two bars and a restaurant.

🛏 ❚ *see pages 104, 127*

19 MARS INN

Loftus, Tees Valley

The **Mars Inn** is a cheerful pub serving all-day drinks and snacks.

❚ *see page 104*

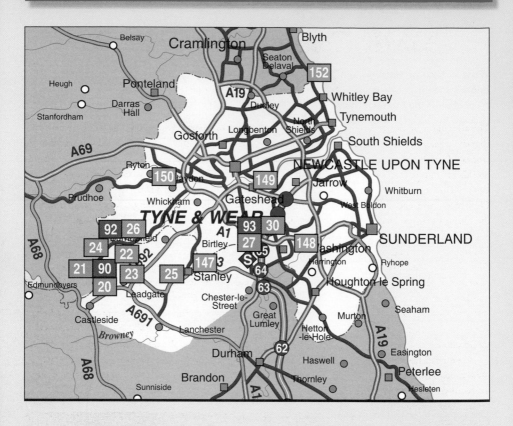

North County Durham with Tyne & Wear

The area south of the Tyne is largely industrial in character, encompassing the large towns and cities of Gateshead, Sunderland and South Shields in Tyne & Wear and, further out in County Durham, the smaller communities of Chester-le-Street and Consett. There is plenty for the visitor to see, particularly in Gateshead and Sunderland, which, like so many large British conurbations, are re-discovering themselves and their heritage. The coastline is a dramatic landscape of beaches, limestone cliffs and headlands. Awarded Heritage Coast status in 2001, a scenic attraction is the Durham Coastal Footpath - an 11-mile clifftop route from Seaham to Crimdon.

Gateshead lies immediately south of Newcastle, on the banks of the River Tyne, and in recent years both have benefited from a tremendous amount of regeneration work. In Gateshead this has revolutionised the riverside area, with such attractions as the Gateshead Millennium Bridge and Baltic Arts Centre.

To the east, South Shields is an area associated with a famous writer. The town is now well established as Catherine Cookson Country, with a Catherine Cookson Trail and a Catherine Cookson Exhibition in the local museum. The origins of

Christianity can be explored in Jarrow, where the Venerable Bede lived and worked as a monk. Sunderland, to the south, is one of England's newest cities, and has the first minster to be created in England since the Reformation. Sunderland is undergoing a reformation of its own. Once an industrial centre the city is thriving again, boosted by the opening in 2002 of a link with Tyneside's Metro system. Attractions include the Sunderland Museum, with its recently refurbished Winter Gardens, and the National Glass Centre.

The area inland from the north bank of the Tyne was an important focus of the Industrial Revolution and the region is steeped in tradition and hard work. Local people – often referred to as Geordies – were employed in the coal mines, engineering works and shipyards. They didn't

Souter Lighthouse, South Shields

travel far to spend their leisure time or holidays, heading for the likes of Whitley Bay or Tynemouth, eight miles east of Newcastle city centre on the North Sea coast, but a lifetime away from their harsh living and working conditions. Today, much of that industry has now gone but the pride and passion remains, as 21st century life, leisure and industry have injected a new vibrancy in the air.

Dominating the region is Newcastle-upon-Tyne, one of Britain's most up and coming cities. An ambitious regeneration programme has transformed the city; stroll down Grey Street one of the most elegant streets in Europe; enjoy the view of the Tyne bridge from the Quayside; visit one of several superb museums and be sure to sample the legendary nightlife. There is a real buzz in the air. Away from Newcastle there are areas of rural calm and beauty waiting to be explored. To the west, and actually in Northumberland, stand the romantic ruins of Prudhoe Castle (see Chapter 5). One of the North East's greatest sons – George Stephenson – was born in Wylam, a village to the west of Newcastle in Northumberland. One room of the small stone cottage where he was born in 1781 is open to the public, but his story is told in greater detail in the Stephenson Railway Museum in North Shields. Legacies of the past can be explored at Segedunum Roman fort, Wallsend – so called because this was where Hadrian's Wall ended; it is now the beginning (or end) of the new Hadrian's Wall National Trail.

---

20 BRADLEYS TEA & COFFEE SHOP

Middle Street, Consett

Bradleys is a spacious first-floor tea and coffee shop serving snacks and meals Monday to Saturday.

 see page 104

21/90 THE CROWN & CROSSED SWORDS

Shotley Bridge, nr Consett

The **Crown & Crossed Swords** is a fine old pub. Bar open all day. Good food. Bed & Breakfast.

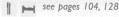 see pages 104, 128

23 THE JOLLY DROVER

Leadgate, nr Consett

The **Jolly Drover** is a modernised 17th century coaching inn open all day for food and drink.

see page 105

CONSETT

Steel-making first started in this area of County Durham at Shotley Bridge, when craftsmen from Germany set up their furnaces in the 17th century and began making swords and cutlery. When the railway came here to serve the local iron works and surrounding collieries in the 19th century, Shotley Bridge began to develop something of a reputation as a spa town, and its popularity as such is evident from the many fine houses to be seen here, such as Dial House.

Steel-making on a grand scale began in Consett in 1840, when the Derwent Iron Company built two blast furnaces. By 1890 over 7,500 people were employed in the industry, and over 1 million tonnes of steel were being produced. In the late 1960s, 6,000 people were still employed in the steelworks, though this wasn't to last. The demand for steel dropped, and in 1980 the works closed forever.

Land reclamation schemes have smartened up the area where the steelworks once stood, and its attendant spoil heaps have made way for green hillocks dotted with young trees. The countryside outside the town has some interesting places to visit.

A redundant railway line north of the town is linked to The Derwent Walk Country Park. The park covers 425 acres of woodland and riverside meadow, and the Derwent Walk itself is the track bed of the old Derwent Valley Railway between Consett and Swalwell. The main walk is 11 miles long, and suitable also for cycles, horses and wheelchairs. It gives access to a number of paths which include nature trails, the South Tyne Cycleway and the Heritage Way. Swalwell Visitor Centre, situated at the northern end of the Derwent Walk, is the starting point for a history trail and has a large pond and butterfly garden. There is another visitor's centre at Thornley Woodlands.

The local council has produced a small guidebook outlining various walks - none more than six and a half miles long - near the town. To the south west of Consett, almost in the North Pennines, is Allensford Park. It sits off the A 68, on the County Durham and Northumberland border, and on the banks of the Derwent. It has a picnic park, caravan site and woodland walks. Deneburn Wood, a ten acre plot of woodland with some delightful walks, also contains wood carvings by well known sculptor, David Gross.

To the south of the town is Hownsgill Viaduct, constructed in 1857 to take the track of the Stanhope and Tyne Railway. Visitors can now walk across it, and there are some spectacular views.

AROUND CONSETT

EBCHESTER

3 miles N of Consett on the A694

Ebchester is the site of a Roman fort called Vindomora, and some scant remains can be seen in the churchyard of St Ebba's Church. It was one of a string of forts on Dere Street, the Roman road which linked York with the north. Inside the church are a number of inscribed Roman stones, including an altar to the god Jupiter, 'the greatest and the best'. Inside the church is the tomb of R S Surtees, creator of Jorrocks, probably the leading character in fox-hunting fiction.

CHESTER-LE-STREET

Chester-le-Street is a busy market town built around the confluence of Cong Burn and the River Wear. There was a Roman fort here at one time, and the street on which the town once stood was a Roman

| 22 | THE ROYAL OAK |

Medomsley, nr Consett

Major refurbishment and an emphasis on food are transforming the **Royal Oak**, a late 18th century inn close to Consett and Shotley Bridge.

see page 104

| 24 | THE DERWENT WALK INN |

Ebchester

Good real ales, hearty home cooking and great valley views are the main attractions at the **Derwent Walk Inn**.

see page 105

Snods Edge, near Consett

road, later replaced by the Great North Road.

The medieval St Mary's and St Cuthbert's Church is built on the site of a cathedral established in AD 883 by the monks of Lindisfarne carrying the body of St Cuthbert. His coffin rested here for 113 years until the monks took it to its final resting place at Durham. There are no fewer than 14 effigies (not all of them genuine) of members of the Lumley family within the church, though they don't mark the sites of their graves. Next to the church is the **Ankers House Museum**, situated in the medieval anchorage. Between 1383 and 1547, various anchorites, or Christian hermits, lived here.

Lumley Castle, to the east across the River Wear, was built in 1389 by Sir Ralph Lumley, whose descendant, Sir Richard Lumley, became the 1st Earl of

Scarborough in the 1690's. In the early 18th century it was refashioned by the architect Vanbrugh for the 2nd Earl, and turned into a magnificent stately home. But gradually the castle fell out of favour with the Lumley family and they chose to stay in their estates in Yorkshire instead. For a while it was owned by Durham University before being turned into the luxurious hotel that it is today.

Waldridge Fell Country Park, two miles south-west of Chester-le-Street and close to Waldridge village, is County Durham's last surviving area of lowland heathland. A car park and signed footpaths give access to over 300 acres of open countryside, rich in natural history.

AROUND CHESTER-LE-STREET

BEAMISH

4 miles NW of Chester-le-Street on the A693

The award-winning **Beamish, The North of England Open Air Museum** is situated in 300 acres of beautiful County Durham countryside and vividly illustrates life in the North of England in the early 1800s and 1900s. This is one of the North East's leading tourist attractions. Buildings from throughout the region have been brought to Beamish, rebuilt and furnished as they once were. Costumed staff welcome visitors and demonstrate the past way of life. Tel: 0191 370 4000.

St Mary & St Cuthberts Church, Chester le Street

Two miles to the northwest is Causey Arch, reputed to be the world's first single-arch railway bridge. It was designed by Ralph Wood, a local stonemason, and carried the Tanfield Railway - opened in 1725 - between Sunniside and Causey. In those days the wagons were pulled by horses, though steam power eventually took over. Trains now run along three miles of line between Sunniside and East Tanfield. There is a car park and picnic area close by, and rights of way link them to Beamish.

SUNDERLAND

Sunderland's history is told in an exhibition in **Sunderland Museum** on Burdon Road. Displays take the visitor back in time to discover the region's proud heritage in textile traditions and coal. Other exhibits include a large collection of Sunderland Pottery and a display of paintings by LS Lowry, who spent much of the last 15 years of his life in the region, finding inspiration for his work in the industrial cities and their coastline. The original Winter Gardens, badly damaged in the 2nd World war, have been re-created - a green oasis in a glass rotunda, with exotic plants from all over the world. The Museum and the Winter Gardens are contained within Mowbray Park, which has been fully restored with themed walkways, poetry inscriptions, historical monuments, a lake and a bowling green. The award winning

Northern Gallery for Contemporary Art is on the top floor of the City Library and on Ryhope Road, south of the city centre, is the university-owned Vardy Art Gallery.

The Exchange Building, the oldest public building in the city, has recently been refurbished, and is now a venue for the whole community to enjoy. Exhibitions, meetings and functions take place there, plus there is a restaurant and café. The famous Empire Theatre - a Sunderland institution – attracts all the top productions.

On the north side of the Wear, in the suburb of Monkwearmouth, is St Peter's Church, one of the most important sites of early Christianity in the country. This tiny Saxon church was founded in AD 674 by Benedict Biscop, a Northumbrian nobleman and thane of King Oswy, who had travelled to Rome and was inspired to found a monastery on his return. This was to become a great centre of culture

147 BEAMISH MUSEUM

Beamish, nr Chester-le-Street

An award winning open air museum illustrating life in the 1800s and 1900s

 see page 148

River Wear, Sunderland

and learning, rivalled only by Jarrow. The Venerable Bede, England's first great historian, lived and worked at St Peter's Church for a time and described the monastery's foundation in his *Ecclesiastical History of England*. The west tower and the wall of this most fascinating church have survived from Saxon times and the area around the church, where shipyards once stood, has been landscaped.

Close by, in Liberty Way, is the **National Glass Centre**. Glass was first made in Sunderland in the 7th century at St Peter's Church, so it's fitting that the centre was built here. Visitors can see how glass was made all those years ago, and watch modern glass blowing. There is a Glass Gallery, devoted to all forms of glass art, and in the Kaleidoscope Gallery there are several interactive exhibits showing glass's many amazing properties. Walking on the roof is not for the faint hearted, as it's made of clear glass panels 30 feet above the riverside. However, some panels are opaque, so people who don't have a head for heights can still walk there and enjoy the view.

Art of another kind is to be found in the St Peter's Riverside Sculpture Trail. It was established in 1990, and comprises various works of outdoor sculpture – in metal, wood, glass and stone - placed along the banks of the Wear - mostly on the Monkwearmouth side.

Monkwearmouth Station is one of the most handsome small railway stations in the British Isles. Built in imposing neo-classical style, it looks more like a temple or a town hall. Trains no longer call here, and it has been converted into a small museum of the Victorian railway age.

Roker is one of Sunderland's suburbs, located to the north of the great breakwaters that form the city's harbour. The northern breakwater, known as Roker Pier, is 825 metres long and was opened in 1903. Roker Park has been carefully restored to its former Victorian splendour, and from Roker and Seaburn through to Sunderland there is a six-mile-long seaside promenade. Crowds of people gather here in July to witness front line jet fighters and vintage planes in action during the Sunderland International Air Show. Tel: 0191 553 2000. On Old Washington Road, the **North East Aircraft**

Roker Pier, Sunderland

Museum houses a collection of aircraft and aero engines, including a Vulcan bomber.

On Newcastle Road, **Fulwell Windmill** is the only working windmill in the North East. Built in 1808, it has been restored to full working order and has a visitor centre. Tel: 0191 516 9790

St Andrew's Church in Talbot Road, Roker, has been described as 'The Cathedral of the Arts and Crafts Movement'. Built by E S Prior in the early 20th century, it is crammed with treasures by the leading craftsmen of the period - silver lectern, pulpit and altar furniture by Ernest Gimson, a font by Randall Wells, stained-glass in the east window by H A Payne, a painted chancel ceiling by Macdonald Gill, stone tablets engraved by Eric Gill, a Burne-Jones tapestry and carpets from the William Morris workshops.

AROUND SUNDERLAND

PENSHAW

4 miles W of Sunderland off the A183

This mining village is famous for the Penshaw Monument - a fanciful Doric temple modelled on the Temple of Theseus, and built in 1844 in memory of the John George Lambton, 1st Earl of Durham and Governor of Canada. A waymarked circular walk of just over three miles links Penshaw Monument with the River Wear.

All Saints Church dates from 1745, and has one unusual feature. Inside it there is a monument to the

Eliot family carved on a piece of stone from the Pyramid of Cheops in Egypt.

To the west is Lambton Castle, scene of an old tale about The Lambton Worm. Legend has it that many years ago, the heir to the Lambton estate was fishing in the Wear one Sunday morning when he should have been at worship. Instead of a fish, he caught a huge worm, which he promptly threw into a well, where it grew to an enormous size. The worm became so big that it could coil itself around hillsides, and began to terrorise the neighbourhood. Meanwhile the heir, away in the Holy Land fighting in the Crusades, knew nothing of this. On his return he met a witch who told him the secret of how the worm could be killed, on the premise that having done so he must then kill the first living thing he met on returning to his village. If he failed to do so the family would be cursed and no Lambton would die peacefully in his or her bed for nine generations. His father, hearing of this, released an old dog close by. Unfortunately, having successfully slain the worm, the young heir didn't see the old dog but his father first, he refused to kill him and the witch's prophesy about the next nine generations came true.

SEAHAM

4 miles S of Sunderland on the B1287

Seaham was developed by the Marquises of Londonderry. In 1821 the family bought what was then the old village of Seaham, in

The *Ryhope Engines Museum* is within the old Ryhope Pumping Station, three miles south of Sunderland city centre. The station was built in 1868 and combines what was then cutting edge technology with functional yet elegantly simple architecture. Tel: 0191 516 0212

order to build a harbour from which to transport coal from the family's collieries to London and the Continent. The present town grew up around the harbour, and although most of the collieries have now closed, Seaham is still very much a working town.

All that now remains of the original village is St Mary the Virgin Church (some parts of which date from Saxon times), its vicarage, and Seaham Hall on the northern outskirts of the town. This was once the home of the Milbanke family, where in 1815 Lord Byron met and married Anne Isabella Milbanke - a marriage that was to last for only one year.

There is a fine sandy beach in Seaham and a sculpture trail running between the harbour and Seaham Hall celebrating the town's heritage.

A major feature of the coast is the **Durham Coastal Footpath**, an 11-mile route that runs from Seaham northwards to Crimdon. It passes through dramatic clifftop scenery and deep ravines carved into the Magnesian limestone rock.

WASHINGTON

6 miles W of Sunderland on the A1231

Present-day Washington is a new town with modern districts scattered over a wide area surrounding the town centre. Built to attract industry into an area whose mining industry was in decline, the town has achieved its aim. The architecture is largely uninspiring, though within the old village of Washington to the east of the town centre, there is one attraction well worth visiting - Washington Old Hall, the ancestral home of the Washington family, ancestors of George Washington, the first American president.

The Hall was originally a manor house built in the 12th century for the de Wessington family, whose descendants through a female line finally left the house in 1613, when it was acquired by the Bishop of Durham.

The present house, in local sandstone, was rebuilt on the medieval foundations in about 1623. In 1936 it was to be demolished, but a hastily formed preservation committee managed to save it, thanks to money from across the Atlantic. In 1955 it was officially reopened by the American Ambassador, and two years later it was acquired by the National Trust.

Washington Old Hall

The interiors re-create a typical manor house of the 17th century, and there are some items on display which are connected to George Washington himself, though the man never visited or stayed there. A peaceful stroll can also be enjoyed in the formal Jacobean garden. Tel: 0191 416 6879

Washington is also the home to the **Washington Wildfowl and Wetlands Trust** – a conservation area and bird watchers' paradise covering some 100 acres of ponds, lakes and woodland sloping down to the River Wear. There are over 1,000 birds representing 85 different species, including mallard, widgeon, nene (the state bird of Hawaii), heron, Chilean flamingos, redshank and lapwing. The Glaxo Wellcome Wetland Discovery Centre has displays and interactive exhibits, hides, a waterfowl nursery and a Waterside Café.

GATESHEAD

For generations Gateshead lived very much in the shadow of neighbouring Newcastle, but no longer. Today the city is at the heart of an impressive regeneration programme that has revitalised the area. In a bid hosted jointly with Newcastle, the city was shortlisted for Capital of Culture 2008, narrowly missing out to Liverpool in the final stage.

Visitors arriving in the city from the South are greeted by one of North East England's most important modern icons - The Angel of the North. Commissioned

Angel of the North, Gateshead

by Gateshead Council and created by renowned sculptor Antony Gormley, this vast and most impressive statue, made from 200 tonnes of steel, is 65 feet high and has a wingspan of 175 feet. Erected in February 1998, the statue has attracted worldwide attention.

Nowhere is the city's transformation more evident than on the Gateshead Quays, a major new arts, leisure and cultural venue on the banks of the River Tyne. One of the most spectacular attractions in Gateshead is the £21 million **Gateshead Millennium Bridge**, erected across the Tyne in 2001 and designed to take both cyclists and pedestrians. A tilting mechanism enables the bridge to pivot at both ends, forming a gateway arch, underneath which ships can pass. This operation, which has been likened to a giant blinking eye, is an engineering

148 WASHINGTON WILDFOWL & WETLANDS CENTRE

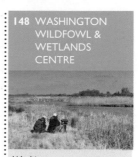

Washington

A fantastic family day out at a centre dedicated to the conservation of the natural habitat of wetland birds.

🏛 *see page 148*

31

River Tyne, Gateshead

149 GATESHEAD MILLENIUM BRIDGE

Gateshead

The world's only tilting bridge creates a stunning display especially when in operation High-tech lighting creates a dazzling show at night.

see page 149

world first for which the bridge has received many accolades. The bridge is particularly impressive at night when it is lit by a high tech, multi-colour light display.

The **Baltic Centre for Contemporary Arts** is a major new international centre for Contemporary art, housed in a converted 1950s grain warehouse. It is one of the largest temporary art spaces in Europe: five galleries display an ever changing programme of work from resident artists. There is also a viewing platform with spectacular views of the Tyne Bridge. Admission is free. Next to the Baltic is the open air performance square, Baltic Square, a venue for street artists and musical events.

Further along the Quayside, in a spectacular Norman Foster building, is **The Sage Gateshead** music centre. The venue boasts a

1650-seat performance hall, 450-seat secondary hall and a school of music, as well as being home to the Northern Sinfonia orchestra. It caters for all tastes – jazz, classical, folk and rock. Linking the Baltic with the Sage Gateshead is a leisure complex with an 18 screen cinema, bowling alley, nightclubs, fitness suites and restaurants.

The Gateshead Quay Visitor Centre is housed in the former St Mary's parish church, a grade I listed church with Norman origins. It includes a display on Gateshead's history and future development plans and a tourist information centre.

Shipley Art Gallery first opened to the public in 1917 and houses a nationally renowned collection of contemporary craft. Also on display is William C Irving's painting of the *Blaydon Races*. The song of the same name, written by Geordie Ridley, a Victorian music hall singer, has become the folklore anthem of Tyneside. When the painting was first exhibited, in the window of an art dealer's shop in Newcastle, it drew such crowds that the police were forced to ask the dealer to draw the blinds.

Saltwell Park is an elegant Victorian park dating back to the 13th century that has impressive floral displays. Gateshead has achieved some notable successes in Britain in Bloom competitions, and in June Gateshead Central Nursery hosts a major flower show.

The Metro Centre is an impressive shopping and leisure complex that is popular with locals and visitors to the area.

AROUND GATESHEAD

GIBSIDE CHAPEL

6 miles SW of Gateshead on the A694

The large mansion at Gibside Estate was owned by the Bowes family, and partially demolished in 1958. Now the place is chiefly visited for the Palladian Gibside Chapel, owned by the National Trust. Building work began in the 18th century but it wasn't until 1812 that the chapel was finally consecrated.

A stately building, looking more like a small mansion than a church, Gibside was built for Sir George Bowes, whose mausoleum lies beneath it. For viewing times call 01207 541820. The Georgian Pleasure Grounds, open daily, have miles of walks through the wooded slopes and riverside of the Derwent Valley. The newly conserved Stables and Orangery opened in July 2005.

JARROW

4 miles E of Gateshead on the A184/A194

Mixed memories surround the town of Jarrow. Once a thriving centre for the Tyneside shipbuilding industry, it gained fame during the famous Jarrow Hunger March when hundreds of unemployed men from the area walked to London to draw attention to their plight. A bas-relief at the Metro Station commemorates the event, which took place in 1936, as does a sculpture outside Morrison's Supermarket.

MARSDEN

9 miles E of Gateshead on the A183

The coast between South Shields and Roker is magnificent, with rocky cliffs projecting into the sea at Lizard Point and the impressive Marsden Bay. Marsden Rock was once a famous County Durham landmark - a rock formation shaped like the Arc de Triomphe that stood in the bay. In 1996, however, it finally succumbed to the forces of nature and collapsed, leaving two tall stumps. The smaller stump proved so unstable that in 1997 it was demolished. The Rock has a famous bird colony of kittiwakes and cormorants. The caves, which were once home to smugglers, have been transformed into a bar and restaurant.

Souter Lighthouse at Lizard Point was built in 1871, and was the first reliable electric lighthouse in the world. It's a perfect example of Victorian technology, and features an engine room, foghorns and lighthouse keeper's living quarters. Owned by the National Trust, and open to the public. Tel: 0191 529 3161. **The Leas**, in the care of the Trust, is a 2½-mile stretch of spectacular coastline running from Trow Rocks to Lizard Point; it includes Marsden Bay, Marsden Rock and many grottoes and sea stacks.

Jarrow has a propitious entry in history books. During the 7th century, Northumbria was a kingdom in its own right, and a shining beacon of learning and Christianity. Bede's World is a museum and outdoor interpretation centre where visitors can explore the extraordinary life of the Venerable Bede. It encompasses both a monastery and church, founded in the 7th century and dedicated to St Paul by Benedict Biscop. The original dedication stone of St Paul's Church can still be seen within its chancel, showing the date of 23 April AD 685, together with fragments of Anglo-Saxon stained glass which scientific tests have established to be the oldest ecclesiastical stained glass in Europe, if not the world. It was at Jarrow monastery, that Bede wrote his famous Ecclesiastical History of England. He was undoubtedly Britain's first genuine historian, employing methods of checking and double checking his information that are still in use today. Jarrow Hall is a Georgian building which has been incorporated into the museum, which also contains a re-created Anglo-Saxon farm.

SOUTH SHIELDS

8 miles E of Gateshead on the A184/A194

South Shields stretches out along the southern shore of the Tyne estuary. Though close to Newcastle and Gateshead, the North Sea coastline here is remarkably unspoiled, and can be walked along for many miles. No less a personage than King George V declared that the beach at South Shields was the finest he had seen. This is a stretch of fine firm sand, behind which a small but pleasant resort thrives.

However, it is the older part of South Shields that has given the town a new claim to fame, thanks to the work of one of the world's most popular novelists - Dame Catherine Cookson, who died in 1998. She was born Katie McMullen in 1906, in a house in Leam Lane amid poverty and squalor, the illegitimate child of a woman called Kate Fawcett. The house is gone now, but a plaque has been erected marking the spot.

Catherine Cookson wrote a series of best-selling novels which captured the world of her own childhood, and that of her parents and grandparents, with vivid clarity. It was a world that was shaped in the 19th century around the narrow streets and coal mines - a world of class warfare and conflict, passion and tragedy, violence and reconciliation.

A **Catherine Cookson Trail** has been laid out in the town, showing places associated with her and her books, and a leaflet is available to guide you round. The South Shields Museum, which recently underwent a major redevelopment, includes an enhanced Catherine Cookson's gallery and an Arts Adventure Centre.

In Baring Street you can see the extensive remains of the 2nd century Roman fort, **Arbeia**. The West Gate has been faithfully reconstructed to match what experts believe to be its original appearance, with two three-storey towers, two gates and side walls. It is the biggest reconstruction of its kind in the country, and a truly magnificent achievement. It also incorporates the Commander's Accommodation and Barracks.

Town Hall, South Shields

Much of the old harbour at South Shields has been restored, particularly around the Mill Dam which is home to the Customs House offering a cinema, theatre, art galleries and an excellent Italian restaurant. Fine Georgian buildings and warehouses still survive in this area along the riverside.

SPRINGWELL

3 miles S of Gateshead on the B1288

Springwell is home to the **Bowes Railway**, once a private rail system pulling coal-filled wagons from pit to port. The original wagonways would originally have been made of wood, with horses pulling the wagons. The line finally closed in 1974, and today the site is a Scheduled Industrial Monument, the only one of its type in the country. The railway is home to a magnificent collection of around 80 colliery wagons, many of them actual Bowes Railway stock, including some former Stockton & Darlington wagons bought secondhand from the North Eastern Railway.

Many of the buildings of the original Springwell Colliery have been retained, as well as the hauliers' houses at Blackham's Hill, where there are demonstrations of the only preserved working inclines in the country, designed and built by George Stephenson. The railway organises special events and open days, and a passenger service operates between the museum centre at Springwell and Wrekenton, with an intermediate stop at Blackham's Hill. Tel: 0191 416 1847

Sandhaven Beach, South Shields

NEWCASTLE-UPON-TYNE

Newcastle, the region's capital, is rapidly becoming one of Britain's most exciting cities, and contains many magnificent public buildings and churches. Situated above the River Tyne, it is linked to its neighbour Gateshead as one visitor destination.

The Tyne Bridge has long been the icon by which Newcastle is internationally known. Opened in 1928, it bears an uncanny resemblance to the Sydney Harbour Bridge, which isn't surprising as both were designed by the same civil engineering company.

Newcastle has enjoyed a varied and colourful history and in its time has acted as a Roman frontier station, a medieval fortress town, an ecclesiastical centre, a great port, a mining, engineering and

30/93 THE BOWES INCLINE HOTEL

Birtley, S of Gateshead

The **Bowes Incline Hotel** offers all the amenities of a fine hotel, a restaurant and a bar.

⊨ ‖ see pages 106,129

35

Tyne Bridge

The city centre is compact, lying mostly within a square mile, so it is easy and rewarding to explore on foot. For the most part the streets are wide and spacious, and like the later Quayside developments after the great fire of 1855, much of the architecture is in the Classical style. During the 17th and early 18th centuries, Newcastle was a major coal port, with its core - still basically medieval in layout - near the riverside. But by the late 1700s the city began moving north, and in the early 1800s architects like William Newton, John Stokoe and John Dobson began designing some elegant Georgian buildings and spacious squares.

Grainger Town, the historic centre of Newcastle, contains many fine examples of classical Victorian architecture. It was designed by Richard Grainger from 1834 with architects John Dobson, John Wardle and George Walker. Up until recently the area was in a state of physical and economic decline but it has been restored to its former splendour by the Grainger Town Project, just one of the examples that epitomises the renaissance of the city. Of particular interest is the Edwardian Central Arcade with its mosaic paving.

Grey's Monument, an 18th century landmark dedicated to the former Prime Minister Earl Grey, stands at the head of Grey Street, about which John Betjeman wrote that "not even Regent Street in London, can compare with that subtle descending curve". With over 40% of its buildings officially

•

Thanks to the Metro Rapid Transport System, Newcastle City and its surroundings are closely linked. It is the second largest underground rail network in Britain linking South Shields and Gateshead, to the south of the city, with the northern coastal areas of Tynemouth and Whitley Bay. It also links up with Newcastle International Airport and takes just 20 minutes to get to the city centre. In 2002 the system was extended to Sunderland, 15 miles away, creating a regional network that can compete with some of the major underground and rapid transport systems in Europe.

•

shipbuilding centre and a focal point of the Industrial Revolution that was to change the face of the world.

The Quayside is the first view of Newcastle for visitors from the south, whether travelling by road or rail. The area is the symbolic and historic heart of this elegant city and boasts some 17th-century merchants' houses mingling with Georgian architecture, and the beautiful Guildhall conatins a state of the art visitor information centre. It has been a focal point for activity since the first bridge was built across the river in Roman times and has been revitalised in recent years with some sensitive and imaginative restoration of the river front area. There are now a number of lively cafés and wine bars along with a regular Sunday market.

To the west of the Quayside is Central Station, designed by local architect John Dobson and officially opened by Queen Victoria in 1850.

listed, Grey Street was awarded the title of Britain's favourite street by listeners to the Radio 4 *Today* programme.

The **Castle Keep** at Castle Garth was built by Henry II in the 12th century on the site of the 'new castle', built in 1080 by Robert, eldest son of William 1, on the site of the Roman fortifications of Pons Aelius. This earlier wooden castle, from which the city takes its name, is thought to have been the start of Hadrian's Wall before it was extended east. It was built after uprisings against the new Norman overlords that followed the killing of Bishop Walcher in Gateshead at a meeting to discuss local grievances.

Henry's impressive new structure was built entirely of stone, and reached 100 feet in height. Although the battlements and turrets were added in the 19th century, much of it is Norman. The only other remaining castle building is Black Gate, dating back to 1247. If at first glance the structure looks a little unusual, it is because of the house built on top of it in the 17th century. The castle was in use during the Civil War, when it was taken by the Scottish army after the Royalist defeat at the Battle of Newburn, five miles west of Newcastle, in 1640.

Many of the other medieval buildings were demolished in the mid-19th century to make way for the railway, and the Castle and Black Gate were fortunate to survive.

At one time, Newcastle was surrounded by stout walls that were 20 to 30 feet high in places and seven feet thick. Parts of these survive and include a number of small towers, which were built at regular intervals. Begun in 1265, the walls were eventually completed in the mid-14th century. They were described as having a "strength and magnificence" which "far passeth all the walls of the cities of England and most of the cities of Europe". The best remaining sections are the West Walls behind Stowell Street, and the area between Forth Street and Hanover Street, south of Central Station, which leads to spectacular views of the River Tyne from the gardens

A notable addition to the city is the Blue Carpet, a pedestrian public square outside the Laing Art Gallery, constructed from purpose made blue glass tiles that attracted considerable controversy when first unveiled. It is just one of over a hundred pieces of public art that can be found at locations across the city. The Gallery houses many paintings, including works by the Northumbrian-born artist John Martin.

Civic Centre

Market by the Guildhall, Newcastle-upon-Tyne

Newcastle is a city that is renowned for its shopping, attracting weekend trippers from as far afield as Scandinavia. Eldon Square contains department stores, restaurants, pubs and cafés, bus and Metro stations, and a sports and recreation centre. The adjoining Eldon Garden is smaller, with a number of specialist shops and designer brands in a stylish environment.

perched on the cliff side.

One unusual feature of the walls was that they passed right through the grounds of a 13th century Dominican monastery, known as Blackfriars, causing the prior to protest loudly. To keep the peace, a door was cut through to allow the monks access to their orchards and gardens. Blackfriars was later converted and turned into almshouses for the destitute. Earmarked for demolition in the 1960s, the building was eventually saved. The church is long gone, but the remaining buildings have been renovated and opened as a craft

centre and restaurant grouped around a small square. It's another of the area's hidden places, and well worth a visit.

Newcastle has two cathedrals - the Anglican **St Nicholas's Cathedral** on St Nicholas Street, and the Roman Catholic **St Mary's Cathedral** on Clayton West Street. St Nicholas, dating from the 14th and 15th centuries, was formerly the city's parish church, and it still has the feel of an intimate parish church about it. Built in 1844, St Mary's was one of A W H Pugin's major works; the spire he originally designed was never built, and the present one dates from 1872.

This is a metropolitan city of great vibrancy and activity, and there's plenty to do, with a rich variety of entertainment on offer. There is a choice of theatres, cinemas, concert venues and an opera house.

The city boasts a wide range of museums and art galleries: The **Discovery Museum**, Blandford Square, depicting Newcastle's social and industrial past; the Laing Art Gallery; the **Hancock Museum**, Barras Bridge - the region's premier Natural History museum, with a magnificent collection of birds, mammals, insects, fossils and minerals; the **Life Science Centre**, Times Square – genetic science brought to life; the **Hatton Gallery**, Newcastle University Art Dept – a permanent collection of West African sculpture; the **Museum of Antiquities**, King's Road; the **Shefton Museum**, Newcastle University – Greek Art and Archaeology; the **Side Gallery**, The Side – documentary photography exhibitions; the Military Vehicle Museum, a collection of World War II and other vehicles housed in the only remaining pavilion of the 1929 exhibition; and the Newburn Hall Motor Museum, Townfield Gardens – a private collection of vintage vehicles.

Down near the quayside is a unique group of half-timbered houses known as **Bessie Surtees House**, owned by English Heritage. The rooms are richly decorated with elaborate plaster ceilings, and there is some beautiful 17th century wall panelling.

To the west of the city, on the south bank of the Tyne, is **Blaydon**, famous for its races, which inspired one of Newcastle's anthems, *The Blaydon Races*. But horse racing hasn't been held here since 1916, and the racecourse is no more. Gosforth Park, to the north of the city, is where horse racing now takes place (Tel: 0191 222 7849 for details of race days). Near Blaydon is the Path Head Water Mill, a restored 18th century mill.

Newcastle is a true Northern capital – a proud city that doesn't look to the South for inspiration and guidance. There is an unmistakable air of confidence in the future. Along with neighbouring Gateshead, Newcastle staged a bid to become European City of Culture 2008. Narrowly missing out to Liverpool in the final stages, the city has none the less been designated as a Centre of Cultural

St Nicholas Cathedral

Excellence with a wide range of events planned for the coming years.

And they've got Michael Owen!

EAST OF NEWCASTLE-UPON-TYNE

NORTH SHIELDS

5 miles E of Newcastle on the A193

Standing at the mouth of the River Tyne the town is named after the shielings (fishermen's huts) on the riverbank. The **Fish Quay**, dating back to 1225, grew up when fishermen were called upon to

150 PATH HEAD WATER MILL

Blaydon

An 18th century water mill, still in the process of being restored. An interesting day out to learn about the power of water.

🏛 see page 149

Worth a visit in North Shields is the Stephenson Railway Museum in Middle Engine Lane. George Stephenson began his career as a humble engine-man at Willington Ballast Hill, before moving to Killingworth where he eventually became an engine-wright. He was the engineer on the world's first passenger rail line - the Stockton to Darlington railway, opened in 1825. The museum remembers the man and his achievements, as well as explaining railway history in the area. Tel: 0191 200 7146

supply Tynemouth Priory. While the boats are smaller in number than in its heyday the port is still a hive of activity, the best time to see fishing boats come into port and experience the hustle and bustle of the landing of catches is between 6 and 7pm. Fabulous fresh fish can be bought from the numerous fishmongers. Many of the buildings on the Fish Quay are linked to the fishing industry. The 'High' and 'Low' lights are prominent landmarks on the upper and lower banks of the Fish Quay that were designed to guide vessels entering the Tyne.

WALLSEND

3 miles E of Newcastle on the A193

In Wallsend the mighty shipyards tower over **Segedunum Roman Fort and Museum** on Buddle Street. The fort was the last outpost on Hadrian's Wall. Segedunum (which means 'strong fort') stood at the eastern end of the Hadrian's Wall. Originally the wall only went as far as Newcastle, but it was decided to extend it to deter sea attacks. There are only scant remains of the structure in the district nowadays.

Segedunum is a reconstruction of what the Roman fort would have looked like. Over 600 Roman soldiers could have been garrisoned here at any one time, and the area must have been a bustling place. Now visitors can explore the reconstructed fort, get a stunning view from a 114-feet viewing tower, and watch archaeologists uncovering yet more foundations of the original wall.

TYNEMOUTH, WHITLEY BAY AND CULLERCOATS

8 miles E of Newcastle on the A193

These three towns form a linked resort. Nestling at the mouth of the River Tyne, Tynemouth boasts a proud maritime heritage. In 1864 the first Volunteer Life Brigade was created here (still in operation today), and visitors can learn more about this vital service in the small museum attached to the lifeboat station. Overlooking the river is the notable **Collingwood Monument**, the grand statue of Admiral Lord Collingwood, Nelson's second-in-command at Trafalgar, who went on to win the battle after Nelson's death. The four guns below the statue are from his ship, the *Royal Sovereign*. Tynemouth Priory was built over the remains of a 7th century monastery, which was the burial place of St Oswin, King of Deira (the part of Northumbria

Priory Ruins, Tynemouth

south of the Tees), who was murdered in AD 651. The priory was as much a fortress as a monastery, which explains the existence of the adjoining 13th century castle ruins. Tynemouth station is the venue for a popular antique market held every weekend. The Palace building on Grand Parade at Tynemouth is home to the **Childhood Memories Toy Museum**, where over 4,000 toys are on display. Tel: 0191 259 1776

Tynemouth Castle

Long Sands is an award winning and gloriously sandy beach that stretches from Tynemouth to Cullercoats, a small town renowned for its history of salt production. In the 1700s around 2180 tons of salt were gathered here each year, abandoned caves were once the hiding place of smugglers who made their fortune illegally transporting it to Scotland. Much quieter than the neighbouring resorts of Tynemouth and North Shields, Cullercoats was a favourite retreat of the famous American artist Winslow Homer, who painted some of his finest works here.

The seaside resort of Whitley Bay has a unique atmosphere at weekends and bank holidays when young people from all over the country come to sample its legendary nightlife. The town has some excellent safe beaches and in July hosts the Whitley Bay International Jazz Festival.

On a small island, easily reached on foot at low tide, is **St Mary's Lighthouse**. The reward for climbing the 137 steps to the top is magnificent views of the Northumberland coast. Completed in 1898, the Lighthouse remained in operation until 1984, when it was superseded by modern navigational techniques. North Tyneside council now runs the Lighthouse and former keeper's cottages as a visitor centre and nature reserve.

SEATON SLUICE

8 miles NE of Newcastle on the A193

Inland from Seaton Sluice is **Seaton Delaval Hall**. This superb Vanburgh mansion, the ancestral home of the Delavals, was built in the Palladian style in 1718 for Admiral George Delaval. Gutted by fire in 1822, it was never restored. Tel: 0191 237 1493. In the grounds of the house stands the Norman St Mary's Chapel.

152 ST MARY'S LIGHTHOUSE

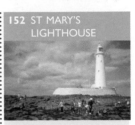

Whitley Bay

A **smart redbrick pub serving some of the best food in the area, with Adnams and Fullers ales to accompany.**

🏛 see page 151

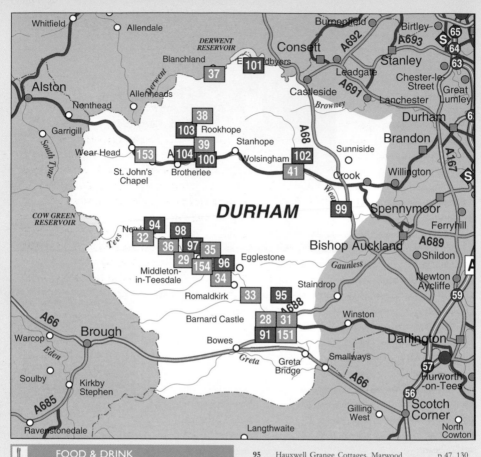

FOOD & DRINK

28	Penny's Tea Rooms, Barnard Castle	p 46, 106, 128
29	The Country Style Bakery & Tea Rooms,	
	Middleton-in-Teesdale	p 49, 106
31	The Raby Arms Hotel, Barnard Castle	p 45, 107
32	High Force Hotel, Forest-in-Teesdale	p 50, 107, 129
33	The Red Lion Hotel, Cotherstone	p 48, 108
34	The Rose & Crown, Mickleton	p 48, 108, 130
35	Teesdale Hotel, Middleton-in-Teesdale	p 49, 108, 130
36	The Strathmore Arms, Holwick	p 50, 109, 131
37	The White Monk Tearoom, Blanchland	p 52, 109
38	The Rookhope Inn, Rookhope	p 54, 109, 133
39	The Cross Keys Inn, Eastgate	p 54, 109, 131
41	The Bay Horse Hotel, Wolsingham	p 55, 110, 132

ACCOMMODATION

91	Penny's Tea Rooms, Barnard Castle	p 46, 106, 128
94	High Force Hotel, Forest-in-Teesdale	p 50, 107, 129
95	Hauxwell Grange Cottages, Marwood	p 47, 130
96	The Rose & Crown, Mickleton	p 49, 108, 130
97	Teesdale Hotel, Middleton-in-Teesdale	p 49, 108, 130
98	The Strathmore Arms, Holwick	p 50, 109, 131
99	Edge Knoll Farm Cottages, Hamsterley	p 50, 131
100	The Cross Keys Inn, Eastgate	p 54, 109, 131
101	Burnside Cottages, Edmundbyers	p 52, 131
102	The Bay Horse Hotel, Wolsingham	p 55, 110, 132
103	The Rookhope Inn, Rookhope	p 54, 109, 133
104	Rose Hill Farm, Eastgate	p 54, 133

PLACES OF INTEREST

151	Bowes Museum, Barnard Castle	p 46, 150
153	The Weardale Museum & High House Chapel,	
	Ireshopeburn	p 53, 151
154	High Force Waterfall, Middleton-in-Teesdale	p 49, 151

42

Weardale, Teesdale & the Pennines

To the west, County Durham sweeps up to the Northern Pennines – a hauntingly beautiful area of moorland, high fells and deep, green dales. Officially designated as an Area of Outstanding Natural Beauty in 1988, the North Pennines covers almost 2,000 square kilometres. It is one of the most remote and unspoiled places in the country and has been called 'England's last wilderness'.

The great northern rivers of the Wear, the Tees, the Tyne and the Derwent have their sources here. Tumbling mountain streams have cut deep into the rock, creating the impressive waterfalls of Low Force, High Force, and Cauldron Snout. These are magical places, and show just how water has shaped the Durham Dales. The area is rich in wildlife. Hen harriers, merlins and other rare species breed here, and in spring and summer the plaintive call of the curlew can be heard.

This is ideal country for walking and cycling, though in the winter months it can be wild and inhospitable. There are numerous rights-of-way to be explored, including the C2C (Coast to Coast) cycle path. The Pennine Way cuts through County Durham in the south, close to the towns of Barnard Castle and Middleton-in-Teesdale, continuing westward through Upper Teesdale until it enters Cumbria. Further north it enters Northumberland to the west of Haltwhistle and then the Northumberland National Park.

Man has left his mark here too, for this is working countryside. The lower reaches have been farmed for centuries, and the high fells are home to many flocks of sheep. At one time there were woollen mills in Barnard Castle, providing a ready market for local sheep farmers. Lead mining was a thriving industry, with mines located at Killhope, Ireshopeburn and St John's Chapel. Middleton-in-Teesdale was once the headquarters of the London Lead Company, a great Quaker business venture.

Teesdale

43

Upper Weardale with the Pennines in the Distance

There are two great County Durham dales - Teesdale to the south and Weardale to the north. Of the two, Teesdale is the softer, particularly in its lower reaches, which share an affinity with the Yorkshire Dales. This isn't surprising, for at one time part of the River Tees formed the boundary between County Durham and Yorkshire. The lower Dale is dotted with charming villages that nestle along the bank of the River Tees, as it winds its way between the historic towns of Barnard Castle and Middleton-in-Teesdale. Small farmsteads, whitewashed in the local tradition, are surrounded by dry stone wall enclosures. Travelling up the dale the vista opens out into miles of open moorland, home to a multitude of wildlife and unique flora. Beyond Middleton-in-Teesdale the B6277 winds up and over some bleak but beautiful scenery until it arrives at Alston in Cumbria, England's highest market town.

The A689, which winds its way through Weardale further north, follows an alternative route to Alston, passing through a dale that was once the hunting ground of Durham's Prince Bishops. Life, at one time, must have been harsh here and the houses and villages seem grittier somehow than those of neighbouring Teesdale. The scars on the landscape expose the regions past as one of the most heavily industrialised upland landscapes in England. Farming developed hand in hand with mining, as the miners supported their variable income with produce from their smallholdings. Methodism was very strong within the communities and many former Methodist chapels can still be seen in the area. There is however plenty to see here, such as the lead mining museum at Killhope, the curious fossilised tree stump at Stanhope, and the village of Blanchland, a few miles to the north in Derwentdale.

BARNARD CASTLE

This historic market town is a natural centre for exploring Teesdale and the Northern Pennines. Set beside the River Tees, 'Barney' is recognised nationally as one of the 51 most historically and architecturally important towns in Great Britain. The town derives its name from Barnard Castle, founded in the 12th century by Bernard, son of Guy de Baliol, one of the knights who fought alongside William I. The castle played an important role in the defeat of the Northern Earls who rose against Elizabeth I in 1569. Besieged by rebel forces for 11 days, the castle was ultimately forced to surrender, but not before its resistance had provided time for Queen Elizabeth's army, under the Earl of Sussex, to speed to York and force the rebels to flee. Many were executed and those leading families who had supported the plans to overthrow Elizabeth I lost their lands.

The castle ruins, with the imposing round keep overlooking the River Tees, have a gaunt beauty. Riverside walks wind through the woods that once formed part of the castle's hunting grounds. County Bridge, a narrow arched bridge built in 1569, traverses the fast flowing River Tees close to the Castle. It formerly spanned the boundaries of two counties and the lands of two bishops, and illicit weddings were regularly conducted in the middle of the bridge, where neither bishop could object.

The town has an especially rich architectural heritage, with handsome houses, cottages, shops and inns dating from the 17th to the 19th centuries. The octagonal Market Cross is a most impressive building, which dates back to 1747 and has served numerous purposes such as courthouse, town hall and jail. Underneath the veranda (a later addition) a lively butter market took place. You can still see the bullet holes in the weather-vane, resulting from a wager by two local men in 1804, shooting from outside the

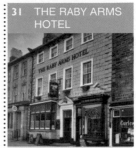

31 THE RABY ARMS HOTEL

Market Place, Barnard Castle

The **Raby Arms** is a great place to meet and eat in historic Barnard Castle, with a wide-ranging menu for all tastes.

see page 107

Castle Ruins

Market Place, Barnard Castle

Penny's is a popular tea room that also has B&B bedrooms.

 see pages 106, 128

Barnard Castle

A wonderful building, housing the superb collection of works of art, gathered by John and Josephine Bowes in the 19th century.

see page 150

Turk's Head, 100 yards away, to determine who was the best shot. The building was fully restored in 1999.

The Bank was once the town's main commercial street and you can still see several Victorian shop windows. Blagraves House is the oldest inhabited building and it is here that Oliver Cromwell is reputed to have sojourned in 1648. The house is now a restaurant, and the locality is an excellent centre for antiques collectors. At the bottom of the Bank glimpses of the town's industrial roots can still be found in Thorngate and Bridgegate. Weavers' cottages have been converted into modern dwellings and grassy slopes cover the remains of riverside woollen mills.

A walk along Newgate will bring visitors to the **Bowes Museum**, one of County Durham's great surprises and surely one of the most spectacular buildings in England. This magnificent French-style château was the inspiration of John Bowes, son of the Earl of Strathmore, and Joséphine, his French actress wife. The designer of the Bowes building was a Frenchman, Jules Pellechet, who apparently took his inspiration from the grand Town Hall in Le Havre. The couple's love of the arts and a desire that people from all walks of life should be able to partake in such riches resulted in this superb legacy. Sadly both died before their dream could be realised, but the museum was completed and opened to the public in 1892. Today the museum houses one of England's finest art collections including paintings by Canaletto, Goya and Turner, as well as fine textiles, ceramics, clocks and watches and antique furniture. A diverse programme of temporary exhibitions running throughout the year complements permanent displays (Tel 01833 690606 for details). The most famous and best loved exhibit is undoubtedly the Silver Swan, a 230-year-old, beautifully crafted life-size mechanical bird that appears to pick up and swallow a fish to the backdrop of a tinkly music box. Set in 23 acres of parkland, the museum boasts a splendid parterre garden; a Tree Trail in the grounds

High Street, Barnard Castle

highlights unusual trees from around the world.

AROUND BARNARD CASTLE

GRETA BRIDGE

4 miles SE of Barnard Castle on the A66

Lovers of romantic landscape should make their way south of Barnard Castle to Greta Bridge on the A66 - the graceful old bridge immortalised in paintings by great English water-colourists such as Cotman and Turner. Footpaths run by the riverside, through the edge of Rokeby Park. Close by are the ruins of medieval Mortham Tower, subject of Sir Walter Scott's narrative poem of colourful chivalry and courtly love, *Rokeby*. The elegant Palladian house, where Scott stayed to write his poem, is open to the public during the summer months. Charles Dickens travelled up the Great North Road from London with his illustrator Hablot K Browne to gather material for his third novel *Nicholas Nickleby*, and they spent their first night in Greta Bridge (see also under Bowes).

EGGLESTONE ABBEY

2 miles S of Barnard Castle, near the A66

South East of Barnard Castle the road leads over an old pack horse bridge to Egglestone Abbey. It is made up of

the ruins of a Premonstratensian abbey of which most of the nave and chancel, built in the 13th and 14th century, survives. Close by is the Meeting of the Waters where the river Greta joins the River Tees, creating splendid views.

BOWES

4 miles W of Barnard Castle off the A66

The ruined Norman castle of Bowes was built on the site of a Roman fort, guarding the approach to Stainmore Pass. In 1838 Charles Dickens visited the village to collect material for *Nicholas Nickleby*, and noticed a boys' academy run by William Shaw in the main street. The school became the model for Dotheboys Hall and Shaw was immortalised as Wackford Squeers. Shaw is buried in the churchyard of St Giles' Church along with George Taylor, Dickens's inspiration for Smike. "I think," Dickens later said, "his ghost put Smike into my head upon the spot."

Packhorse Bridge, Egglestone Abbey

47

33 THE RED LION HOTEL

*Cotherstone,
nr Barnard Castle*

The **Red Lion** is a classic village pub open every evening and Saturday lunchtime. Food served weekend evenings.

¶ see page 108

39 THE ROSE & CROWN

*Mickleton,
nr Middleton-in-Teesdale*

The **Rose & Crown** is a locals pub and a fine base for touring Teesdale, with B&B rooms and a caravan site.

¶ ⊨ see pages 108, 130

Three miles west of Bowes on the A66 is the **Otter Trust's North Pennines Reserve**, a 230-acre wildlife reserve with British and Asian otters and bird hides overlooking wetland areas. The otters are fed at noon and 3pm daily. Tel: 01833 628339

ROMALDKIRK

4 miles NW of Barnard Castle on the B6277

Between Middleton and Barnard Castle, the B6277 follows the south bank of the River Tees passing through pretty unspoiled villages such as Cotherstone and Romaldkirk. The church at Romaldkirk, known as the Cathedral of the Dales, is dedicated to the little-known St Romald or Rumwald, son of a Northumbrian king who could miraculously speak at birth. Beautiful stone houses are set around spacious greens and there are delightful walks close to the river.

EGGLESTON

6 miles NW of Barnard Castle on the B6281

Within the grounds of Eggleston Hall are **Eggleston Hall Gardens**, which are open to the public all year. There are four acres of garden here within the high wall that once enclosed the kitchen garden. The ornamental gardens are laid out informally, with many rare herbaceous plants and shrubs to be seen. Vegetables are cultivated using the traditional organic methods.

MIDDLETON-IN-TEESDALE

10 miles NW of Barnard Castle on the B6277

Middleton-in-Teesdale, the capital of Upper Teesdale, is a small town in a dramatically beautiful setting with the River Tees running below, while all around is a great backcloth of green hills, within the North Pennines Area of Outstanding Natural Beauty. The town's links with the lead-mining industry can be seen in the Market Square, where there is a handsome cast-iron fountain which was purchased and placed there in 1877 by the employees of the Quaker-owned London Lead Mining Company. The expense was covered from subscriptions raised for the retirement of the company's local superintendent, Robert Bainbridge.

Village Green, Middleton-in-Teesdale

Low Force Waterfall, nr Middleton-in-Teesdale

29 THE COUNTRY STYLE BAKERY & TEA ROOMS

Market Place, Middleton-in-Teesdale

Visitors to the **Country Style Bakery & Tea Rooms** can enjoy an all-day selection of hot and cold snacks, pastries and gluten free cakes.

see page 106

35/97 TEESDALE HOTEL

Market Square, Middleton-in-Teesdale

The **Teesdale Hotel** is the ideal base for exploring an area rich in scenic and historic interest.

see pages 108, 130

154 HIGH FORCE WATERFALL

Middleton-in-Tessdale

A pretty woodland walk will lead you to this spectacular waterfall with its 70 feet drop.

see page 151

At the west end of Hude is Middleton House, the company's former headquarters.

Although the lead-mining industry disappeared at the beginning of the 19th century, Middleton still retains the strong feeling of being a busy working town. The surrounding hills still bear the scars, with the remains of old workings, spoil-heaps and deep, and often dangerous, shafts. The town's agricultural links remain strong, with streets bearing names such as Market Place, Horsemarket and Seed Hill. **Meet the Middletons**, on Chapel Row, is an excellent interpretation of life in the area in the 1800s, with family-friendly interactive displays.

Like Barnard Castle, it is increasing in popularity as a centre from which to explore Teesdale and the Northern Pennines. Middleton is the centre for some magnificent walks in Upper Teesdale. The most famous of these is The Pennine Way, which passes through the town on its 250-mile route from Derbyshire to Kirk Yetholm in Scotland. Turning west along Teesdale the track passes through flower-rich meadows, traditional, whitewashed farmsteads and spectacular, riverside scenery, including the thrilling waterfalls at Low Force, High Force and Cauldron Snout.

The majestic **High Force** is England's largest waterfall in terms

*Holwick,
nr Middleton-in-Teesdale*

Fine food, real ales and comfortable B&B rooms add to the glorious scenery at the **Strathmore Arms**.

🍴 🛏 *see pages 109, 131*

*Forest-in-Teesdale,
nr Barnard Castle*

The celebrated **High Force Hotel** is a perfect base for a relaxing stay amid the wonderful scenery of the region.

🛏 🍴 *see pages 107, 129*

Hamsterley, nr Bishops Auckland

Edge Knoll Farm Cottages are an ideal base for a walking, touring or sporting holiday.

🛏 *see page 131*

of water flow, with a dramatic 21-metre drop over Great Whin Sill at the end of a wooded gorge. After heavy rainfall its rumble can be heard over a mile away. **Low Force** isn't so much a waterfall as a series of cascades, and whilst less spectacular than its upstream neighbour, it is equally beautiful. Further up the Dale from High Force is Cow Green Reservoir and below it Cauldron Snout, which cascades down dolerite steps. A nature trail leads from Cow Green car park to Cauldron Snout and Moor House Nature Reserve, home to some rare Alpine plants, including the Blue Gentian.

About three miles northwest of Middleton-in-Teesdale, near the village of Newbiggin, is the **Bowlees Visitor Centre**, where information on the natural history and geology of the area is displayed. The picnic area has four small waterfalls and a footpath to Gibson's Cave and Summerhill Force.

HAMSTERLEY FOREST

9 miles N of Barnard Castle off the A68

Hamsterley Forest is one of the Forestry Commission's most attractive Forest Parks. This huge area encompassing over 5,500 acres of mature woodland is managed for timber production, and has 1,100 acres available for recreation. A wide range of activities are on offer for visitors including informal or guided walks, orienteering, horse-riding and cycling (bikes can be hired). There is a visitors centre with displays on forestry, wildlife

and timber usage, and large, grassy areas make splendid picnic spots.

Surprisingly enough, the Forest is largely artificial and relatively recent in origin, having been planted only 40-50 years ago. Much of it covers areas once worked by the lead-mining industry. This is a good area to discover a range of wild flowers and, in the damper places, fungi. Red squirrels can still be seen in the forest, along with roe deer, badgers, adders and up to 40 species of birds including heron, woodcock, sparrow hawk, woodpeckers, fieldfare and goldfinch.

STANHOPE

Stanhope, the capital of Upper Weardale, is a small town of great character and individuality, which marks the boundary between the softer scenery of lower Weardale and the wilder scenery to the west. The stone cross in the market place is the only reminder of a weekly market held in the town by virtue of a 1421 charter. The market continued until Victorian times, but today the town continues to serve the surrounding villages as an important local centre for shops and supplies.

Enjoying an attractive rural setting in the centre of the Dale, with a choice of local walks, Stanhope, in its quiet way, is becoming a small tourist centre with pleasant shops and cafés. Stanhope enjoyed its greatest period of prosperity in the 18th and 19th centuries when the lead

250 Million Year Old Fossil Tree, Stanhope

One of the most important Bronze Age archaeological finds ever made in Britain was at Heathery Burn, a side valley off Stanhope Burn. In 1850, quarrymen cut through the floor of a cave to find a huge hoard of bronze and gold ornaments, amber necklaces, pottery, spearheads, animal bones and parts of chariots. The treasures are now kept in the British Museum.

and iron-stone industries were at their height, as reflected in the town's buildings and architecture.

The most dominant building in the Market Square is **Stanhope Castle**, a rambling structure complete with mock-Gothic crenellated towers, galleries and battlements. The building is, in fact, an elaborate folly built by the MP for Gateshead, Cuthbert Rippon in 1798 on the site of a medieval manor house. In 1875 it was enlarged to contain a private collection of mineral displays and stuffed birds for the entertainment of Victorian grouse-shooting parties. In the gardens is the **Durham Dales Centre**, which contains the Tourist Information centre, a tea room and a sculptured children's animal trail. The Dales Garden was first developed as an exhibit at the Gateshead National Gardens Festival in 1990 and has

been re-created here using typical Dales cottage garden plants.

St Thomas's Church, by the Market Square, has a tower whose base is Norman, and some medieval glass in the west window. In the churchyard is a remarkable fossil tree stump which was discovered in 1962 in a local quarry.

The **Weardale Railway** runs for five miles between Stanhope and Wolsingham in the North Pennines Area of Outstanding Natural Beauty. Subject to availability, the trains are steam-hauled. Call 01845 600 1348 for timetable details.

Stanhope Old Hall, above Stanhope Burn Bridge, is generally accepted to be one of the most impressive buildings in Weardale. This huge, fortified manor house was designed to repel Scottish raiders. The privately owned hall itself is part medieval, part

Elizabethan and part Jacobean. The outbuildings included a cornmill, a brew house and cattle yards.

AROUND STANHOPE

ALLENHEADS

9 miles NW of Stanhope on the B6295

Allenheads also has lead-mining connections, with its scatter of stone miners' cottages and an irregular village square with pub and chapel in a lovely setting. The village is a centre for fine, upland rambles through the surrounding hills, which still retain many signs of the former industrial activity. From Allenheads the main road climbs over Burtree Fell into Weardale, with wild moorland roads branching across to Rookhope to the east and Nenthead to the west.

BLANCHLAND

7 miles N of Stanhope on the B6306

A small, serene estate village on the Northumberland and Durham border. This is another of the area's hidden places, and one well worth seeking out. The name Blanchland (white land) comes from the white habits worn by the canons of the Premonstratensian Order who founded Blanchland Abbey in 1665. The abbey was dissolved by Henry VIII in 1537. In 1702, Lord Crewe, the Bishop of Durham bought the Blanchland estate. On his death in 1721 the estates were left to the Lord Crewe Trustees who were responsible for building the picturesque village of Blanchland which you see today, using stone from the ruined Abbey buildings.

Blanchland

Small cottages snuggle round a village square opposite the popular Lord Crewe Arms, housed in part of the priory next to the ancient abbey church of St Mary the Virgin.

COWSHILL

8 miles W of Stanhope on the A689

In a hollow between Cowshill and Nenthead lies **Killhope Mine**. The Pennines have been worked for their mineral riches, lead in particular, since Roman times but until the 18th century the industry remained relatively primitive and small scale.

Old Lead Mining Works, Killhope

Mechanisation in the late 18th and early 19th century allowed the mining industry to grow until it was second only to coal as a major extractive industry in the region. Now the country's best-preserved lead-mining site, Killhope Mine is the focal point of what is now the **North of England Lead Mining Museum**, dominated by the massive 34-feet water wheel. It used moorland streams, feeding a small reservoir, to provide power for the lead ore crushing mills, where the lead ore from the hillside mines was washed and crushed ready for smelting into pigs of lead. Much of the machinery in the Museum has been carefully restored by Durham County Council over recent years, together with part of the smelting mill, workshops, a smithy, tools and

miners' sleeping quarters. Winner of The Guardian Family Friendly Museum Award for 2004.

FROSTERLEY

3 miles E of Stanhope on the A689

The village is famous for Frosterley marble, a black, heavily fossilised limestone that in former times was used extensively for rich decorative work and ornamentation on great public and private buildings throughout the north. The Chapel of the Nine Altars in Durham Cathedral makes extensive use of Frosterley Stone, sometimes called Durham Marble.

IRESHOPEBURN

8 miles W of Stanhope on the A689

At Ireshopeburn, between Cowshill and St John's Chapel, is the delightful little **Weardale Museum**, situated in the former minister's house next to an 18th

153 THE WEARDALE MUSEUM & HIGH HOUSE CHAPEL

Ireshopeburn

A fascinating collection of Methodist memorabilia and displays illustrating local life in bygone ages.

 see page 151

38/103 THE ROOKHOPE INN

Rookhope, Weardale

The **Rookhope Inn** is a popular village pub with good beer, classic pub food and 5 guest bedrooms.

 see pages 109, 133

39/100 THE CROSS KEYS INN

Eastgate, nr Stanhope

The **Cross Keys** is a fine old inn offering a convivial ambience, home cooking and B&B accommodation.

 see pages 109, 131

104 ROSE HILL FARM

Eastgate, nr Stanhope

Rose Hill Farm is a perfect base for lovers of the outdoor life, and its spacious bedrooms offer every comfort.

see page 133

century Methodist chapel. The exhibits include a carefully re-created room in a typical Weardale lead-miner's cottage kitchen, with period furnishings and costumes, local history and mineral displays, and a room dedicated to John Wesley, who visited the area on several occasions. The museum is open during summer months only.

POW HILL COUNTRY PARK

7 miles N of Stanhope on the B6306

Set in moorland overlooking the Derwent Reservoir, Pow Hill lies on the south shore and has great views of the lake. Conserved for its special wildlife interest, this valley bog habitat is home to goldcrests, coal tits, roe deer and red squirrels. The western end of the lake is protected as a nature reserve. In winter large flocks of migrant waders and wildfowl gather here.

ROOKHOPE

3 miles NW of Stanhope off the A689

Rookhope (pronounced Rook-up), in lonely Rookhope Dale, is on the C2C cycle route, and has a history lost in antiquity, dating back to Roman times.

Another old fashioned Dale village, Rookhope is set in a hidden North Pennine valley. The remains of lead and iron mine activity now blend into quiet rural beauty. At one point the road climbs past Rookhope Chimney, part of a lead-smelting mill where poisonous and metallic-rich fumes were refined in long flues.

ST JOHN'S CHAPEL

7 miles W of Stanhope on the A689

St John's Chapel is named after its parish church, dedicated to St John the Baptist. Like many of the surrounding villages, it was once a lead mining centre and is still the home of an annual Pennine sheep auction in September that attracts farmers from all over the North Pennines. This is the only village in Durham to boast a town hall, a small building dating from 1868 overlooking the village green.

The road from St John's Chapel to Langdon Beck in Teesdale rises to 2,056 feet as it passes over Harthope Fell, making it the highest classified road in England.

WESTGATE AND EASTGATE

4 miles W of Stanhope on the A689

The area between the lovely stone built villages of Westgate and Eastgate was once the Bishop of Durham's deer park, kept to provide him with an abundant supply of venison. The villages are so called because they were the east and west 'gates' to the park. The foundations of the Bishop's castle can still be seen at Westgate along with an old mill and water wheel. In 1327 the troops of Edward III camped at Eastgate en route to Scotland to face the Scottish army.

WOLSINGHAM

5 miles E of Stanhope on the A689

Wolsingham is one of the oldest market towns in County Durham and has its origins in Saxon times.

Westgate

The town has strong links with the iron and steel industries; Charles Attwood who was one of the great pioneers in the manufacture of steel founded the town steelworks, which once cast a variety of anchors and propellers for ships.

Tunstall Reservoir, north of Wolsingham, and reached by a narrow lane, lies in a valley of ancient oak woods alongside Waskerley Beck. The reservoir was built in the mid 19th century, originally to provide lime-free water for the locomotives of the Stockton and Darlington Railway to prevent their boilers from scaling like a domestic kettle. It now forms part of a delightful area to stroll, picnic or go fishing.

41/102   THE BAY HORSE HOTEL

Wolsingham, Weardale

A fine old hotel with 7 guest bedrooms and characterful public areas. The reastaurant serves a wide range of dishes.

 see pages 110, 132

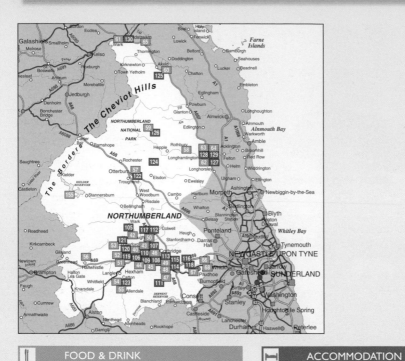

🍴 FOOD & DRINK

🛏 ACCOMMODATION

🏛 PLACES OF INTEREST

Hadrian's Wall & the Northumbrian National Park

West Northumberland, where the North Pennines blend into the Cheviots, is an exhilarating mixture of bleak grandeur, beauty and history. Stretching north towards the Scottish border are the 398 square miles of the Northumbrian National Park and the Kielder Forest Park, while to the south is Hadrian's Wall, that monumental feat of Roman civil engineering built on the orders of Emperor Hadrian in AD 122.

Towards the east of the area, the hills slope down towards a stretch of fertile land with little towns like Rothbury and Wooler, which in themselves deserve exploration. But up on the high ground a person could walk for miles without meeting another soul. The highest point, at 2,650 feet, is the Cheviot itself, a few miles from the Scottish border.

This is the land of the Border Reivers, or mosstroopers, bands of marauding men from both sides of the Border who rustled, pillaged and fought among themselves, incurring the wrath of both the English and Scottish kings. A testament to their activities is the fact they gave the word blackmail to the English language. The 'mail' part of blackmail is an old Scottish word for a tax payment, and blackmail was a payment made by Border farmers to the Reivers as protection money. The Pennine Way passes over the moorland here, dipping occasionally into

View over College Valley, Near Kirknewton

surprisingly green and wooded valleys. There are also less strenuous walks, circular routes and cycle tracks laid out, with maps and leaflets available from the park visitor centres, at Rothbury, the quaintly-named Once Brewed, and Ingram. Here you can also learn about the history of the area as well as things to see.

Blaweariw near Wooler, Overlooking the Cheviot Hills

Three main valleys penetrate the park from the east - Harthope Valley, Breamish Valley and Coquetdale. Harthope Valley is accessed from Wooler, along the Harthope Burn. Part of it is called Happy Valley, and is a popular beauty spot. There are a number of circular walks from the valley floor up into the hills and back again.

Breamish Valley is the most popular of the valleys, and it's here that the Ingram Visitors Centre, open in the summer months only, is located. Again, there are trails and walkways laid out.

Coquetdale is the gentlest of the three, and is popular with anglers. It winds up past Harbottle towards Alwinton and Barrowburn, but in so doing passes through the Otterburn Training Area, where up to 30,000 soldiers a year come to practise their artillery skills. This has actually preserved the upper part of Coquetdale from modern development, and farming here has changed little over the years. The valley is rich in wildlife, and heron, sandpiper and grey wagtail are common. The exposed crags support rock-rose and thyme, and there are patches of ancient woodland.

The Kielder Forest covers 200 square miles, and is situated to the west of the National Park. It contains Europe's largest man-made lake, Kielder Water, opened by the Queen in 1982.

In the south of the National Park is by far the greater part of Hadrian's Wall, the best known Roman monument in Britain, and the best known Roman frontier in Europe. It stretches for 80 Roman miles (73 modern miles) across the country from Bowness-on-Solway in the west to Wallsend in the east, and in 1987 was declared a UNESCO World Heritage Site. A new national trail, the Hadrian's Wall Path runs for 84 miles following the rolling, northern terrain along the entire length of the Wall, and from May to September, the Hadrian's Wall Bus Service runs from Carlisle to Hexham (and Newcastle and Gateshead Metro Centre on a Sunday), stopping at the main attractions along the route. To see the Wall twisting across the moorland is an awe-inspiring site, and no visitor to Northumberland should miss it.

HEXHAM

The picturesque market town of Hexham sits in the heart of Tynedale, and is its capital and administrative centre. It's rich in history and character and an ideal base from which to explore the Tyne Valley and Hadrian's Wall.

Hexham Abbey, one of the most important churches in the north of England, was at one time known as 'the largest and most magnificent church this side of the Alps'. It was founded by St Wilfrid in AD 674 after Queen Etheldreda of Northumbria granted him some land. The crypt of this early church remains almost intact, and access to it is via a stairway from the nave. The crypt was built using Roman stones, and on some of them you can still see inscriptions and carvings. Frith Stool, also known as St Wilfrid's chair, is a 1,300-year-old stone chair that is believed to have been used as a coronation throne for the ancient kings of Northumbria.

In 1130 a group of Augustinian canons set up an abbey on the site. The present church dates from the 13th century and contains some wonderful late-medieval architecture, which later restoration has not diminished. It has a rich heritage of carved stonework, and the early 16th century rood screen has been described as the best in any monastic church in Britain.

The Abbey was ransacked many times by the Scots armies, who at one time poured over the border into England. However, this was a two-way traffic, and the English did likewise to the abbeys at Melrose and Kelso.

The Abbey overlooks the Market Place, where a lively and colourful market is held each

42/105 SIMONBURN TEA ROOMS AND B&B

Simonburn, nr Hexham

Simonburn Tea Rooms and B&B is a pleasant spot for a snack or an overnight stay.

see pages 111, 133

40 THE RAILWAY INN

Fourstones, nr Hexham

Locals and tourists steam along to the **Railway Inn** to enjoy the cheerful ambience, Jennings ales and hearty food.

see page 109

106 THISTLERIGG FARM

High Warden, nr Hexham

Thistlerigg Farm has 3 B&B rooms in a hillside setting that commands spectacular views.

see page 133

Hexham Abbey

43/107 THE HADRIAN HOTEL

Wall, Hexham

A charming stone building, elegantly furnished and offering a varied menu in the restaurant.

see pages 111, 134

44/108 THE ROYAL HOTEL

Priestpopple, Hexham

The **Royal** is a smart, well-run hotel on the main street of Hexham, with an adjacent Indian restaurant.

see pages 111, 134

45/109 THE COUNTY HOTEL

Priestpopple, Hexham

The **County** is a small, friendly, family-run hotel on Hexham's main street.

see pages 111, 134

46/110 THE SUN INN

Acomb, nr Hexham

The **Sun Inn** is both a cheerful 'local' and an excellent choice for a meal or an overnight stay.

see pages 112, 134

47/111 THE ROSE & CROWN

Slaley, nr Hexham

The **Rose & Crown** is a classic village pub offering fine home cooking and smart B&B rooms.

see pages 112, 135

112 THE HERMITAGE

Swinburne, nr Hexham

The Hermitage is a superb country mansion with beautiful guest bedrooms.

see page 135

Tuesday. Nearby is the early 14th century Moot Hall, built of Roman stone. In olden days it served as the courtroom of the Archbishop of York, who held the grand title of Lord of the Liberty and Regality of Hexham. Today the hall houses the **Border History Library**, which contains material on Border life, in particular the music and poetry of the region.

Nearby, the Manor Office was England's first purpose-built prison and was built by the Archbishop in 1332 as a gaol for his courthouse. The **Border History Museum** is located within the gaol and tells, in a vivid way, the story of the border struggles between Scotland and England. For centuries the borderlands were virtually without rule of law, ravaged by bands of men known as Reivers - cattle rustlers and thieves who took advantage of the disputed border lands. Powerful wardens, or Lords of the Marches, themselves warlords of pitiless ferocity, were given almost complete authority by the king to control the Reivers and anyone else who crossed their path. However, for all their power and ferocity they were singularly unsuccessful in controlling the bloodshed. This was the period of the great border ballads, violent and colourful tales of love, death, heroism and betrayal, which have found an enduring place in literature.

The award winning **Queens Hall Arts Centre** with theatre, café, library and exhibitions presents a full and varied

programme throughout the year.

The town of Hexham has retained much of its character, with winding lanes and passageways, attractive 18th and 19th century houses, handsome terraces and some delightful shops and a market. There are some fine gardens around the abbey, and several attractive areas of open space. Tyne Green Country Park features attractive walks along the riverside and a picnic and barbecue site.

Hexham National Hunt Racecourse at Acomb is one of the most picturesque courses in the country. Call 01434 606881 for details of meetings. At Simonburn, just north of Hadrian's Wall, **St Mungo's Church** is the Mother Church of the North Tyne Valley.

AROUND HEXHAM

CORBRIDGE

3 miles E of Hexham on the A69

The lively market town of Corbridge was, for a time, the capital of the ancient Kingdom of Northumbria. The original Roman town, **Corstorpitum**, lay half a mile to the northwest, and was an important military headquarters. Visitors to the site can see the substantial remains of this strategic river crossing, which include a fine example of military granaries and two fortified medieval towers, which are evidence of more troubled times. The museum houses finds from the excavation of the site, the most famous of which is the Lion of Corbridge – a

Corbridge

48/113 DYVELS HOTEL

Corbridge, nr Hexham

Dyvels Hotel is a pleasant, civilised place for a drink, a meal or a comfortable overnight stay.

🍴 🛏 see pages 112, 135

114 THE HAYES

Newcastle Road, Corbridge

Guests staying at **The Hayes** have a choice of B&B and self-catering accommodation.

🛏 see page 136

49/115 THE GOLDEN LION

Hill Street, Corbridge

The **Golden Lion** attracts visitors with fine hospitality, wholesome food and excellent B&B rooms.

🍴 🛏 see pages 113, 136

116 CROOKHILL FARM

Newton, 2 miles E of Corbridge

Crookhill Farm scores high marks for comfortable rooms, lovely views and super breakfasts.

🛏 see page 136

stone fountainhead. The 14th century Vicar's Pele was, as the name implies, formerly the home of the vicar, and the other, Low Hall, dating from the 13th century, was converted into a private house in 1675.

The finest building in Corbridge is undoubtedly St Andrew's Church. It still retains many Saxon features, and the base of the tower was once the west porch of the Saxon nave. Within the tower wall is a complete Roman arch, no doubt removed from Corstorpitum at some time.

Corbridge is also the site of the Northumberland County Show, held each year on the late May Bank Holiday Monday.

AYDON

4 miles E of Hexham off the B6321

Aydon Castle is a superb example of a fortified manor house, such protection being necessary in this region in times past to keep the Reivers at bay. Built by Robert de Reymes in the late 13th century, it remains remarkably intact, and is often described as one of the best preserved fortified manor houses in Britain, thanks to its early owners and now to English Heritage.

CHOLLERFORD

3 miles N of Hexham on the B6318

The Roman fort of **Chesters**, or Cilurnum, to give it its Roman name, is situated in the parkland created by Nathaniel Clayton

118 OVINGTON HOUSE

Ovington, nr Stockfield

Ovington House is a distinguished 18th century country residence with beautifully appointed bedrooms and a self-catering option.

🛏 see page 137

50/117 BARRASFORD ARMS HOTEL

Barrasford, nr Hexham

The **Barrasford Arms Hotel** offers B&B, self-catering and camping-style accommodation close to Hadrians Wall.

🛏 🍴 see pages 113, 136

51/119 THE RAILWAY HOTEL

Church Street, Haydon Bridge

The **Railway Hotel** has a welcome for all, whether it's for a drink, a bite to eat or a weekend break.

🍴 🛏 see pages 113, 137

52/120 HADRIANS LODGE HOTEL

Hindshield Moss, nr Haydon Bridge

Hadrians Lodge Hotel provides everything for a pleasant holiday in historic, scenic surroundings.

🛏 🍴 see pages 113, 137

around the mansion he had built in 1771. The fort covers nearly six acres and was large enough to accommodate a full cavalry regiment. The **Clayton Museum** houses a remarkable collection of Roman antiquities. Remains of the Roman fort include a well preserved bath house and barracks. Near the bath house can be seen the foundations of a Roman bridge that carried a road across the Tyne.

CHOLLERTON

6 miles N of Hexham on the A6079

Chollerton, six miles north of Hexham, enjoys an exceptionally fine setting. Nearby is the site of the **Battle of Heavenfield**, where King (later St) Oswald defeated the army of Cadwalla, a Welsh king.

BARRASFORD

7 miles N of Hexham off the A6079

Barrasford sits on the North Tyne across from **Haughton Castle**, of which there are fine views. The castle is one of the finest great houses in Northumberland, and dates originally from the 13th century. Over the succeeding years, additions and alterations have been made, with the west wing being designed by Anthony Salvin and built in 1876. The castle isn't open to the public.

HAYDON BRIDGE

6 miles W of Hexham on the A69

Two bridges cross the Tyne here - a modern concrete one dating from 1970, and an older one dating from 1776. North of the village is Haydon Old Church, close to

where the medieval village of Haydon lay. It dates partly from the 12th century.

LANGLEY

6 miles W of Hexham on the B6295

Langley Castle, now a hotel and restaurant, was built in around 1350. In 1450, Henry 1V had it destroyed, but it was restored in the 1890s by a local historian, Cadwallader Bates. In the 17th and early 18th centuries the Castle was owned by the Earls of Derwentwater, and in 1716 the third earl, James, was beheaded in London for his part in the 1715 Jacobite rebellion. His brother Charles was later beheaded for his part in the 1745 uprising. A memorial to them sits beside the A686 not far from the castle. Guided tours of the Castle and grounds are available by prior arrangement – Tel: 01434 688888

BARDON MILL

10 miles W of Hexham on the A69

Bardon Mill, a former mining village, stands on the north bank of the South Tyne. An important drovers' road crossed the river here and cattle were fitted with iron shoes at Bardon Mill to help them on their way to southern markets. The village is a convenient starting point for walks along **Hadrian's Wall** and the Roman forts of **Vindolanda** and **Housesteads** are nearby. At Vindolanda excavations continue to reveal fascinating insights into Roman life. An open air museum features a reconstructed temple, shop and

Hadrians Wall

53/121 OLD REPEATER STATION

Grindon, nr Haydon Bridge

The Old Repeater Station provides a choice of accommodation close to Hadrians Wall.

see pages 113, 137

54 THE GOLDEN LION

Allendale, nr Hexham

The Golden Lion is an imposing stone inn serving excellent food every session. Accommodation for 2006.

see page 114

55/123 ALLENDALE TEA ROOMS

Allendale, nr Hexham

Allendale Tea Rooms serve home-cooked food in a friendly, relaxed atmosphere. Also 2 rooms for B&B.

see pages 114, 139

house. Perched high on a ridge, with splendid views of the surrounding countryside, the remains of Housesteads Fort cover over five acres and is one of the finest sections of Hadrians Wall. Nearby, **Once Brewed** is the main Visitor Centre for Hadrians Wall and the Northumberland National Park.

Between Bardon Mill and Haydon Bridge lies the confluence of the South Tyne and the River Allen, which, like the Tyne, comes from two main tributaries - the East Allen and West Allen. The valleys of the East and West Allen really are hidden jewels. The 22,667 acres of Allen Banks, as the lower part of the valley near the Tyne is known, is a deep, wooded, limestone valley, rich in natural beauty, now owned by the National Trust.

ALLENDALE

10 miles SW of Hexham on the B6295

Allendale Town lies on the River East Allen, set against a backdrop of heather clad moorland, and was

Signpost, Haltwhistle

56 THE MILECASTLE INN

Cawfields, north of Haltwhistle

Visitors to nearby Hadrian's Wall will find a friendly welcome, cask ales and super home cooking at the **Milecastle Inn**.

 see page 114

once an important centre of the north Pennine lead-mining industry. It retains attractive houses from prosperous times and a surprisingly large number of existing or former inns around the Market Square. A sundial in the churchyard in Allendale records the fact that the village lies exactly at the mid point between Beachy Head in Sussex and Cape Wrath in Scotland, making it the very centre of Britain.

HALTWHISTLE

15 miles W of Hexham on the A69

The origins of the name Haltwhistle are unknown but two suggestions are the watch (wessel) on the high (alt) mound, or the high (haut) fork of two streams (twysell). It is difficult to imagine that this pleasant little town with its grey terraces was once a mining area, but evidence of the local industries remain. An old pele tower is incorporated into the Centre of Britain Hotel in the town centre. Holy Cross Church, behind the Market Place, dates back to the 13th century and is said to be on the site of an earlier church founded by William the Lion, King of Scotland in 1178, when this area formed part of Scotland.

Three miles northwest of Haltwhistle, off the B6318, is Walltown Quarry, a recreation site built on the site of an old quarry. Today part of the Northumberland National Park, it contains laid-out trails and it is possible to spot oystercatchers, curlews, sandpipers and lapwings.

SLALEY

4 miles SE of Hexham, off the B6306

Slaley is a quiet village consisting of one long street with some picturesque houses dating from the 17th, 18th and 19th centuries. One of the finest houses - Church View - stands opposite the 19th century St Mary's Church. Two miles southwest, Slayley Hall has some interesting gardens.

OTTERBURN

The village of Otterburn stands close to the centre of the National Park, in the broad valley of the River Rede. It makes an ideal base for exploring the surrounding countryside, an exhilarating area of open moorland and rounded hills. It was close to here, on a site marked by the 18th century Percy Cross, that the **Battle of Otterburn** took place in 1388 between the English and the Scots. By all accounts it was a ferocious encounter, even by the standards of the day, and one commentator said that it "was one of the sorest and best fought, without cowards or faint hearts".

Under the command of Earl Douglas, a gathering of Scottish troops at Jedburgh in 1388 had resolved to enter England in a two-pronged attack - one towards Carlisle and one down into Redesdale. In charge of the Redesdale contingent was the Earl of Douglas, who got as far as Durham before being forced back to the border by Henry Percy, better known as Hotspur, and his brother Ralph.

In August the English caught up with the Scottish army at Otterburn, and went straight into attack. The battle continued for many hours, gradually descending into a series of hand to hand fights between individual soldiers. Gradually the Scots got the upper hand, and captured both Percys. But it was a hollow victory, as the Earl of Douglas was killed. A second force under the Bishop of Durham hurried north when it heard the news, but it wisely decided not to engage in battle. A series of markers known as Golden Pots are said to mark the journey

of Douglas's body when it was taken back to Melrose.

There are some interesting walks around Otterburn, and some well preserved remains of Iron Age forts can be seen on both Fawdon Hill and Camp Hill.

North of the village are the remains of **Bremenium** Roman fort. It was first built by Julius Agricola in the 1st century, though what the visitor sees now is mainly 3rd century. In its day the fort could hold up to 1,000 men, and was one of the defences along the Roman road now known as Dere Street. Close by is the **Brigantium Archaeological Reconstruction Centre**, where you can see a stone circle of 4000 BC, Iron Age defences, cup and ring carvings and a section of Roman road.

AROUND OTTERBURN

BELLINGHAM AND WARK

7 miles SW of Otterburn on the B6320

The North Tyne is fed by the Kielder Water, which on its way down to join the South Tyne above Hexham passes by the interesting villages of Bellingham and Wark.

Bellingham (pronounced Bellin-jam) is a small market town in a moorland setting, with a broad main street, market place and the austere little **St Cuthbert's Church**, reflecting the constant troubles of the area in medieval times. To prevent marauding Scots from burning it down, a massive stone roof was added in the early 17th century.

57/122 THE OTTERBURN TOWER HOTEL

Otterburn

Set in beautiful gardens, the **Otterburn Tower Hotel** combines the best qualities of a country house hotel and a top-class restaurant.

see *pages 115, 138*

•

Otterburn Mill dates from the 18th century, though a mill is thought to have stood on the site from at least the 15th century. Although production of woollens ceased in 1976, the mill is still open, and on display are Europe's only original working 'tenterhooks' (whence the expression 'being on tenterhooks'), where newly woven cloth was stretched and dried.

•

124 BEESWING LODGE

Elsdon, nr Otterburn

Self-catering guests at **Beeswing Lodge** enjoy peace and tranquillity in a beautiful rural setting.

see page 139

In the churchyard an oddly shaped tombstone, somewhat reminiscent of a peddler's pack, is associated with a foiled robbery attempt that took place in 1723. A peddler arrived at Lee Hall, a mansion once situated between Bellingham and Wark, and asked if he could be put up for the night. As her master was away at the time the maid refused, but said that he could leave his heavy pack at the Hall and collect it the next day.

Imagine her consternation when some time later the pack began to move. Hearing her screams for help, a servant rushed to the scene and fired his gun at the moving bundle. When blood poured out and the body of an armed man was discovered inside, the servants realised that this had been a clever attempt to burgle the Hall. They sounded a horn, which they found inside the pack next to the body, and when the robber's accomplices came running in response to the prearranged signal, they were speedily dealt with.

Wark, to the south of Bellingham, is an attractive estate village, once part of the lordship of Wark. The Scottish kings are said to have held court here in the 12th century. **Chipchase Castle**, is a combination of 14th century tower, Jacobean mansion and Georgian interior. A walled nursery garden is open to the public throughout the summer months but the castle itself is only open on June afternoons. Tel: 01434 230203

On the slopes overlooking the North Tyne are a large number of unusually named prehistoric settlements, such as Male Knock Camp, Good Wife Camp, Nigh Folds Camp, Carryhouse Camp and Shieldence Camp.

ELSDON

3 miles E of Otterburn on the B6341

The village of Elsdon is of great historical importance. Built around a wide green, with **St Cuthbert's Church** in the middle, it was the medieval capital of Redesdale - the most lawless place in Northumberland, and scene of some of the worst border fighting. In later years it became an important stopping point on the drovers' road.

In the late 19th century, when the church was being

Elsdon

Kielder Water

restored, over 1,000 skulls were uncovered. They are thought to be those of soldiers killed at the Battle of Otterburn.

Elsdon Tower, which in 1415 was referred to as the 'vicar's pele', dates from the 14th century, though it was largely rebuilt at a later date. It is one of the most important pele towers of the region and is now a private residence.

HEPPLE

8 miles NE of Otterburn on the B6341

Hepple has a reminder of the difficulty of life near the borders in the form of **Hepple Tower**, a 14th century pele tower built so strongly that attempts to demolish it and use the stone for a new farmhouse had to be abandoned. West of the village, on the moors, are some fine examples of fortified houses and farms.

KIELDER

16 miles W of Otterburn off the B6320

Kielder village was built in the 1950s to house workers employed in the man-made **Kielder Forest**, which covers 200 square miles to the west of the **Northumberland National Park**.

Here at Kielder Forest you'll find one of the few areas in Britain that is home to more red squirrels than grey, thanks to careful forest planning that ensures a constant supply of conifer preferred by red squirrels. Otters, too, are resident in Kielder, and the area abounds with deer and rare birds and plants.

There's some excellent walking to be had, with several marked trails and routes to suit all abilities, from a leisurely stroll to an energetic climb, with maps and leaflets to guide you round. There are also cycle routes, including the 17 mile Kielder Water Cycle Route, and bicycles can be hired from the local visitors centre.

Within the forest is **Kielder Water**, opened by the Queen in 1982; it is the largest man-made lake in Northern Europe with over 27 miles of shoreline. The visitor can take a pleasure cruise aboard the *Osprey*, an 80-seat passenger cruiser that stops at several points of interest along the lake.

Located at sites around the lake and within the forest is an art and sculpture trail of works inspired by the surroundings. **Leaplish**

155 KIELDER WATER AND FOREST PARK

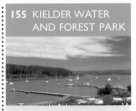

Kielder, Northumberland

A peaceful area offering a wealth of recreational activities including walking, sailing and riding.

🏛 see page 152

High Street, Rothbury

Elm Tree Coffee Shop is open seven days a week for savoury and sweet snacks and hot and cold drinks.

see page 116

High Street, Rothbury

On the main street of Rothbury, the **Turks Head** wins friends for food, drink and accommodation.

see pages 116, 139

Waterside Park has a range of activities and attractions for all ages, including one of the largest and most fascinating collections of birds of prey in the North of England. Tel: 01434 250400

To the northwest is **Kielder Castle**, at one time a hunting lodge for the Duke of Northumberland, and later offices for the Forestry Commission. It is now a fascinating visitor centre with exhibits describing the development of the forest and the birdlife that is found in Kielder.

ROTHBURY

12 miles E of Otterburn on the B6341

The attractive town of Rothbury is a natural focal point from which to explore the valley of the River Coquet. It is an excellent starting point for some delightful walks, either along the valley or through the nearby woodland. The most famous perhaps being the trail to the Rothbury Terraces, a series of parallel tracks along the hillside

above the town.

Simonside, a hill offering a fine viewpoint, is steeped in history and the subject of several legends. Flint arrowheads have been recovered there, as well as bronze swords, shards of pottery, axe heads and ornaments. Burial cairns abound, as do carved stones and ancient paths. The Northumberland National Park has prepared a leaflet, which guides you on a walk up and onto the hill.

To the north of Simonside is Lordenshaws, with a well defined hill fort, Bronze Age burial mounds, rock carvings and cairns.

From the 18th century the village developed into a natural marketplace for Upper Coquetdale, to which cattle and sheep were brought for sale, and the drovers were provided with numerous alehouses. Since the mid 19th century Rothbury has been a holiday resort for walkers and fishermen, and the railway, which opened in 1870, contributed further to its growth. The former Saxon parish church of Rothbury was almost entirely rebuilt in 1850 and it is worth visiting the interior to see the font, which stands on part of the 9th century Rothbury cross.

Just outside Rothbury is the house and estate of **Cragside**, once the home of Sir William Armstrong, arms manufacturer and industrialist. He bought 14,000 acres in the valley of the Debden Burn, and employed architect Norman Shaw to extend the existing house and make it suitable

River Coquet, Rothbury

to entertain royalty and other wealthy guests. Work began in 1864, and what finally emerged in 1884 was a mock-Tudor Victorian mansion. A pioneer of the turbine, Armstrong designed various pieces of apparatus for the house, and devised his own hydroelectric systems, with man-made lakes, streams and miles of underground piping, making Cragside the first house in the world to be lit by hydroelectricity. Cragside is now owned by the National Trust, and has been sympathetically restored to show how upper middle class Victorians were beginning to combine comfort, opulence and all the latest technology in their homes. The house is currently closed for re-wiring but the gardens are open.

Rothbury

WELDON BRIDGE

15 miles E of Otterburn on the A697

Weldon Bridge is an exceptionally elegant bridge across the River Coquet, dating from 1744. Although it no longer carries the main road, it remains an impressive feature.

Nearby is **Brinkburn Priory**, standing in secluded woodland on the banks of the river. It was established in about 1135 by William de Bertram, 1st Baron Mitford, and is thought to have been built by the same masons who constructed nearby Longframlington church. It is in a beautiful setting surrounded by ancient trees and rhododendrons, and was once painted by Turner as a romantic ruin. Its church was

restored in 1859 by Thomas Austin on behalf of the Cadogan family, and has many fine architectural features. It is also the setting for famous annual summer concerts.

LONGFRAMLINGTON

15 miles E of Otterburn on the A697

Longframlington derives its name from its principal family, the de Framlingtons, who are recorded as the 12th-century benefactors of Brinkburn Priory. The route of the Devil's Causeway, a Roman road between Hadrian's Wall and the

62/127 ANGLERS ARMS

Weldon Bridge, Longframlington

The **Anglers Arms** has earned a great reputation as a fine place for a drink, a meal or a relaxing break.

see pages *117, 140*

69

63/128 THE NEW INN

Longframlington, nr Morpeth

The **New Inn** is building a fine reputation for delicious pub food; the same owners offer self-catering accommodation nearby.

  🍴   🛏   see pages 117, 140

64/129 EMBLETON HALL

Longframlington, nr Morpeth

Embleton Hall is a distinguished country house hotel with beautifully appointed bedrooms and a choice of bar and restaurant menus.

  🛏   🍴   see pages 117, 140

60/125 RYECROFT HOTEL

Wooler, North Northumberland

The **Ryecroft** is a family-run hotel on the A697, with 9 en suite bedrooms and good home cooked food and Real Ale

  🛏   🍴   see pages 116, 139

Scottish border, can easily be traced west of the village, along what is now a farm lane past Framlington Villa.

There are few shops here but the village retains the traditional craftsmanship of a Northumbrian pipe maker. The workshop, where you can see the production of these unique and beautiful musical instruments, is open to the public.

WOOPERTON

20 miles NE of Otterburn off the A697

Wooperton is close to the site of the **Battle of Hedgeley Moor**, which took place in 1464. In truth this was more of a skirmish, in which the Yorkist Lord Montague defeated the Lancastrian Sir Ralph Percy, who was killed. The site of the Battle of Hedgeley Moor is marked by a carved stone called the Percy Cross and can be reached along a short footpath leading from the A697.

WOOLER

Wooler is a small town standing on the northern edge of the Cheviots, midway between Newcastle and Edinburgh, and is an excellent centre for exploring both the Cheviots and the border country. In the 18th and early 19th centuries it became an important halt on the main north-south coaching route and is now holds regular markets of sheep and cattle.

There are few outstanding buildings in Wooler, though the town itself makes a pleasing whole.

There are superb walking opportunities in the area surrounding Wooler, for example, the Iron Age hill fort immediately west of the town, Earle Whin and Wooler Common, or via Harthope onto The Cheviot itself. Alternatively, the visitor can take a vehicle into the Harthope Valley with a choice of walks, easy or strenuous, up and through the magnificent hillsides of this part of the Northumberland National Park.

The visitor can also climb **Humbledon Hill**, on top of which are the remains of a hill fort, built about 300 BC. The Battle of Humbledon Hill was fought here in 1402 between the English and the Scots, who had been on a raiding mission as far south as Newcastle. Due to the firepower of Welsh bowmen in the English army, the Scottish army assembled within the fort was easily defeated. Human and horse bones have been uncovered while Humbledon Hill's northern slopes were being

Wooler Town Centre

ploughed, and an area is still known to this day as Red Riggs from the blood, which stained the ground during and after the battle.

KIRKNEWTON

6 miles W of Wooler on the B6351

Kirknewton is a typical border village made up of cottages, a school and village church. **St Gregory's Church** dates mainly from the 19th century, though there are medieval fragments such as an unusual sculpture, which shows the Magi wearing kilts – a fascinating example of medieval artists presenting the Christian story in ways their audience could understand.

Josephine Butler, the great Victorian social reformer and fighter for women's rights, who retired to Northumberland and died here in 1906, is buried in the churchyard. Her father had been a wealthy landowner, and a cousin of British Prime Minister Earl Grey of Howick Hall, near Craster.

Half a mile east of the village, in what are now fields by the River Glen, lay the royal township of Gefrin or Ad-Gefrin, better known as Yeavering. Discovered in 1948 thanks to aerial photography, this was where, in the 7th century, King Edwin of Northumbria built a huge wooden palace that included a royal hall over 100 feet long, storehouses, stables, chapels and living quarters. A stone, and a board explaining the layout, now mark the place where this long-vanished royal establishment once stood.

Site of the Battle of Flodden Field

BRANXTON

8 miles NW of Wooler off the A697

The site of the decisive **Battle of Flodden Field** can be found near Branxton, marked by a cross in a cornfield reached by a short path. It was here that the English army heavily defeated a Scottish army under the command of King James IV on 9th September 1513. The king was killed, and his body lay in St Paul's Church in Branxton, now rebuilt. An information board explains the background to the battle and how it was fought.

CORNHILL-ON-TWEED

10 miles NW of Wooler at the junction of the A697 and A698

An unusual attraction near Cornhill is **Heatherslaw Cornmill**, a 19th century cornmill restored to working order, producing stoneground wholemeal flour. It's open daily from mid-March to the end of September, and in winter Monday, Friday and other dates when milling. Tel: 01890 820338.

•

On the summit of a hill near Kirknewton known as Yeavering Bell is a magnificent Iron Age hill fort, the largest in Northumberland, enclosed by the remains of a thick wall and covering 13 acres. Over 130 hut circles and similar buildings have been traced on the summit, which commands impressive views for miles around.

•

61/130 THE COLLINGWOOD ARMS

Main Street, Cornhill-on-Tweed

The **Collingwood Arms** combines the qualities of a comfortable hotel and a fine restaurant.

see pages 116, 141

71

Etal

Blessed Virgin Mary was built in 1858 by Lady Augusta Fitzclarence in memory of her husband and daughter.

NORTH AND WEST OF NEWCASTLE-UPON-TYNE

WYLAM

5 miles W of Newcastle off the A69

Wylam is the birthplace of George Stephenson, railway pioneer, and one room in the little stone cottage where he was born in 1781 is open to the public.

PRUDHOE

9 miles W of Newcastle on the A695

The romantic ruins of **Prudhoe Castle** are in the care of English Heritage. King William the Lion of Scotland unsuccessfully attacked the castle in 1173 and 1174, and the threat of further attacks led Henry II to agree to the building of a new stone castle. Completed in the 12th century, it was one of the finest in Northumberland, and was later provided with a moat and drawbridge, a new gatehouse and a chapel. There is an impressive oriel window above the altar of the chapel. A Georgian manor house in the courtyard houses an exhibition, which tells the history of the castle. Tel: 01661 833459

MICKLEY SQUARE

10 miles W of Newcastle on the A695

A signpost at Mickley Square points visitors to **Cherryburn**. The house is noted as the birthplace of

---

65   BLACK BULL

Etal Village, Cornhill on Tweed

A delightful white washed, thatched pub with a wealth of rustic charm. Home-cooked Northumbrian food.

🍴 see page 118

66   THE FOX & HOUNDS

Main Street, Wylam

The **Fox & Hounds** is a spotless village pub well known for its good home cooking.

🍴 see page 118

67   THE JIGGERY POKERY

Stocksfield

The **Jiggery Pokery** is a combination of busy tea room and collectables shop.

🍴 see page 118

FORD AND ETAL

4 miles E of Cornhill-on-Tweed on the B6353 (Ford) or B6354 (Etal)

The twin estate villages of Ford and Etal were built in the late-19th century. Ford is a 'model' village with many beautiful stone buildings and well-tended gardens. Dating originally from the 14th century but heavily restored in the 19th, Ford Castle was the home of Louisa Ann, Marchioness of Waterford. In 1860 she built the village school and spent the next 20 or so years decorating it with murals depicting biblical scenes. As models she used local families, thus creating a pictorial gallery of life and work in the area at that time. Now known as **Lady Waterford Hall**, it is open daily in the summer for visits. Etal is an attractive village within which are the ruins of the 14th century castle destroyed by King James IV of Scotland. The **Church of the**

Thomas Bewick, the well-known illustrator and wood engraver, famous for his portrayal of birds, animals and country life. Now owned by the National Trust, the house contains an exhibition of his woodcuts and hosts regular demonstrations of the printing techniques used in his time.   Tel: 01661 843276

BLYTH

12 miles NE of Newcastle on the A193

Blyth is a small industrial town at the mouth of the River Blyth. Much of the town's industrial heritage is linked to the Northumberland coalfields, their rapid decline in recent years is a loss from which the area is only slowly recovering. The oldest part of the town is set around an 18th century lighthouse called the High Light. Blyth claims its own piece of railway history with one of the country's earliest wagonways, the **Plessey Wagonway**, dating from the 17th century and built to carry coal from the pits to the riverside. As well as coal mining and shipbuilding, the town was once a centre of salt production, and in 1605 it is recorded that there were eight salt pans in Blyth. Blyth's industrial landscape and coastline was the inspiration for several paintings by L S Lowry. The building that is now the headquarters of the Royal Northumberland Yacht Club was a submarine base during the Second World War.

Prudhoe Castle

PONTELAND

7 miles NW of Newcastle on the A696

Though this small town has largely become a dormitory town for Newcastle-upon-Tyne, resulting in a lot of recent development, it still retains a character of its own. **St Mary's Church**, much altered but essentially 12th century, stands opposite the attractive Blackbird Inn, housed in a 13th and 14th century fortified house. Within the gardens of the Old Vicarage is a 16th century vicar's pele.

A few miles north of Ponteland are **Kirkley Hall Gardens**, which are open to the public. There are 35,000 different species of labelled plant here, and it is home to the national collections of beech, dwarf willow and ivy.

68   THE RISING SUN

Crawcrook, Tyne & Wear

The **Rising Sun** is a lively pub serving a great selection of home-cooked dishes.

see page 118

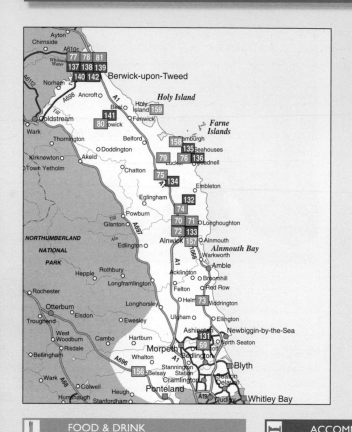

🍴 FOOD & DRINK

🛏 ACCOMMODATION

🏛 PLACES OF INTEREST

The Northumberland Coastal Area

Stretching from the edge of the Cheviots to the East Coast, and from the River Blyth in the south to Berwick-upon-Tweed in the north, this is an area of quiet villages and small market towns, majestic castles, and what many people consider to be the finest coastline in England. Designated as the North Northumberland Heritage Coast, the area boasts a wealth of historical attractions such as Bamburgh Castle, Lindisfarne and the Farne Islands.

For all its beauty, it's a quiet coastline, and you can walk for miles along the dunes and beaches without meeting another soul. No deck chairs or noisy ice cream vans here - just a quietness broken occasionally by the screeching of gulls. Coquet Island is a renowned bird sanctuary where the visitor can see puffins, roseate terns, razorbills, cormorants and eiders.

Lindisfarne, a small island lying between Bamburgh and Berwick, is perhaps the most evocative place of all on the coast. It was to here that St Aidan and a small community of Irish monks came from Iona in AD 635 to found a monastery from which missionaries set out to convert northern England to Christianity.

The region has withstood a tempestuous past and has been the focus of fierce fighting, nowhere more so than the Border town of Berwick, whose strategic location made it a prime target in the endless skirmishes between the English and the Scots. All along the coastline can be seen superb castles; some have been converted into grand mansions for the great families of the area, while others are now no more than ruins.

Inland from the coast the land is heavily farmed, and there is a pleasant landscape of fields, woodland, country lanes and farms. The villages, with their ancient parish churches and village greens, are especially fine. The village green was essential in olden times, as the Scots constantly harried this area, and the villagers needed somewhere to guard their cattle after bringing them in from the surrounding land.

The area to the southeast, around Ashington, was once coal mining country, though the scars are gradually being swept away. The industry is remembered in a museum of mining at Woodhorn. Even here however, an earlier history is evident, as the former Woodhorn church is one of the most interesting in Northumberland.

One of the North East's greatest sons - George Stephenson was born in Wylam, a village to the west of Newcastle. His story is told in the Stephenson Railway Museum, North Shields (see Chapter 2).

Berwick-On-Tweed

MORPETH

The county town of Morpeth seems far removed, both in spirit and appearance, from the mining areas further down the Wansbeck valley. An attractive market town, Morpeth was once a stopping point on the A1 from Newcastle and Edinburgh, before the days of bypasses, and some fine inns were established to serve the former travellers.

The Norman's built a castle here that stood in what is now **Carlisle Park**. It was destroyed by William Rufus in 1095. A second castle was built close by, but was demolished by King John in 1215. It was subsequently rebuilt, but was mostly destroyed yet again by Montrose in 1644. Known as Morpeth Castle, it is now a restored gatehouse, managed by the Landmark Trust and is open once a year.

The third - which isn't really a castle but has the appearance of one - was built by John Dobson in 1828 as the county gaol and courthouse. Still standing, it is now private apartments and self catering accommodation.

The Clock Tower in the middle of Oldgate has been heightened several times. It probably dates from the early 17th century, though medieval stone was used in its construction. In its time it has served as a gaol and a place from where the nightly curfew was sounded. Its bells were a gift from a Major Main, who was elected MP for the town in 1707. He had intended them for Berwick, but they didn't elect him, so, as a local saying goes, "the bells of Berwick still ring at Morpeth". The Clock Tower is one of only a handful of such buildings in England. The Town Hall was built to designs by Vanbrugh, and a handsome bridge over the Wansbeck was designed by Telford.

Not to be missed is the 13th century **Morpeth Chantry** on Bridge Street, one of only five bridge chantries still in existence. Originally the Chapel of All Saints, it has been in its time a cholera hospital, a mineral water factory and

River Wansbeck, Morpeth

a school where the famous Tudor botanist William Turner was educated. Nowadays it houses the museum of the Northumbrian bagpipe - a musical instrument that is unique to the county. The town's tourist Information centre is also located here, as are a craft centre, a picture framers and a mountain sports shop.

St Mary's Church, lying to the south of the river, dates from the 14th century. It has some of the finest stained glass in Northumberland. In the churchyard is the grave of Suffragette Emily Davison, who was killed under the hooves of Anmer, the king's horse, during the 1913 Derby meeting. Her funeral attracted thousands of people to Morpeth. About a mile west of the town are the scant remains of Newminster Abbey, a Cistercian foundation dating from the 12th century. It was founded by monks from Fountains Abbey in Yorkshire.

The Old Courthouse, Morpeth

AROUND MORPETH

WALLINGTON HALL

11 miles W of Morpeth off the B6342

Wallington Hall, lying deep in the heart of the Northumbrian countryside, is a National Trust property dating from 1688. The two great families associated with the place - the Blacketts and the Trevelyans - have each made their own mark on what must be one of the most elegant houses in Northumberland. In the Great Hall

is a famous collection of paintings about Northumbrian history, and one of the rooms has an unusual collection of dolls' houses.

Nearby is the village of Cambo, where the renowned landscapist Lancelot Brown, better known as Capability Brown, was born.

BELSAY

7 miles SW of Morpeth on the A696

Belsay Hall was built for Sir Charles Monck on an estate that already had a castle and a Jacobean mansion. Set in 30 acres of landscaped gardens, Belsay Hall is Greek in style and contains the architecturally splendid Great Hall. Two miles west is the Bolam Lake Country Park, with a 25 acre lake, trails and picnic areas

BEDLINGTON

5 miles SE of Morpeth off the A189

Bedlington, formerly known as the county town of Bedlingtonshire,

69/131 THE ANGLERS ARMS

Choppington, nr Morpeth

The **Anglers Arms** provides cheerful hospitality and five B&B rooms.

see pages 119, 141

156 BELSAY HALL CASTLE AND GARDENS

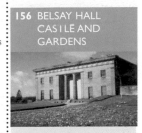

Belsay, near Ponteland

A magnificent grade I hall standing in 30 acres of beautifully landscaped gardens.

see page 152

was a district of the County Palatinate of Durham until 1844, when it was incorporated into Northumberland. The town became the centre of a prosperous mining and iron-founding community and has two important links with railway history. The rolled-iron rails for the Stockton and Darlington Railway were manufactured here, and it is also the birthplace of the great locomotive engineer, Sir Daniel Gooch. One of the greatest engineers of his day, Sir Daniel was the locomotive superintendent on the Great Western Railway, and the man who first linked up North America and Europe via a telegraph line.

There is an attractive country park near Bedlington at Humford Mill, with an information centre and nature trails. At Plessey Woods, south west of the town, another country park extends along the wooded banks of the River Blyth, around Plessey Mill, with trails and a visitor centre.

ASHINGTON
5 miles W of Morpeth on the A197

Ashington is a sprawling town around the River Wansbeck, built to serve the mining industry. The two-mile-long **Wansbeck Riverside Park**, which has been developed along the embankment, offers sailing and angling facilities, plus a four mile walk along the mouth of the River Wansbeck. The famous footballing brothers Bobby and Jackie Charlton were born in Ashington in the 1930s, and the cricketer Stephen Harmison is also a son of the town.

NEWBIGGIN BY THE SEA
7 miles E of Morpeth on the A197

Newbiggin by the Sea is a fishing village and small resort enjoying an attractive stretch of coastline with rocky inlets and sandy beaches, now much improved after the ravages of the coal industry. St Bartholomew's Church has a particularly interesting 13th century interior. The village has the oldest operational lifeboat house in Britain, built in 1851.

WOODHORN
6 miles E of Morpeth on the A197

At Woodhorn, close to Ashington, there is the fascinating late-Anglo-Saxon St Mary's Church, said to be the oldest church building in Northumberland. The outside was heavily restored in 1843, though the inside is almost wholly pre-

Newbiggin by the Sea

Norman. There is a 13th century effigy of Agnes de Velence, wife of Hugh de Baliol, brother of the Scottish king, John Baliol.

The Woodhorn Colliery Museum, which is linked to the Queen Elizabeth Country Park by a short light railway, offers interesting displays of mining life and the social history of the area. 'Turning the Pages' is an award winning, interactive exhibition on the Lindisfarne Gospels.

LONGHORSLEY
6 miles N of Morpeth off the A697

Longhorsley is noted for being the home of Thomas Bell, inventor of self-raising flour. He called it Bell's Royal, but the name was later changed to Bero.

Born at Blackheath in London in 1872, Emily Davison spent a lot of time in the village. A plaque on the wall of the post office, her former home, commemorates her death under the hooves of the King's horse at Epsom in 1913. Her suffragette activities are remembered by the local Women's Institute each year when flowers are placed on her grave in the family grave in Morpeth.

ALNWICK

Alnwick (pronounced Annick) is one of Northumberland's most impressive towns. It still retains the feel and appearance of a great medieval military and commercial centre, being an important market town since the granting of its charter in 1291. The town is dominated by the huge fortress of **Alnwick Castle**, set in beautiful parklands designed and landscaped in the 18th century by Capability Brown and Thomas Call. Alnwick Castle began, like most of Northumberland's castles, as a Norman motte and bailey. In the 12th century this was replaced by a stone castle, which was greatly added to over the centuries. In 1309, the castle came into the possession of Henry de Percy, who strengthened the fortifications. Henry's great grandson was made an earl, and the castle was then passed down 11 generations of Earls. When the male Percy line

70 THE FLEECE INN

Bondgate Without, Alnwick

The **Fleece Inn** is a popular food-and-drink pub with friendly family hosts.

see page 119

71 NARROWGATE RESTAURANT

Narrowgate, Alnwick

Narrowgate Restaurant is a daytime coffee shop/restaurant that becomes an intimate à la carte restaurant Thursday to Sunday evenings.

see page 119

Alnwick Castle

79

157 ALNWICK CASTLE

Alnwick

The impressive medieval castle contains a wealth of history, beautiful grounds and a variety of displays and exhibitions.

 see page 153

72/133 THE ODDFELLOWS ARMS

Narrowgate, Alnwick

In the old part of town right by the Castle, the **Oddfellows Arms** offers good food and drink and comfortable B&B accommodation.

 see pages 120, 141

died out, it passed through the female line to Sir Hugh Smithson, who took the Percy name and was created Duke of Northumberland. When the Duke inherited the castle in 1750 it was falling into disrepair and he commissioned the renowned Robert Adam to restore the castle into a residence fit for a Duke. The superb ceilings and fireplaces can still be seen today. Further sweeping changes were made in the 1850s and 1860s, when the 4th Duke commissioned the Victorian architect Anthony Salvin to transform the castle into a great country house with all modern comforts while recapturing its former medieval glory. Visitors can admire the Italian Renaissance-style State Rooms and treasures that include paintings by Titian, Tintoretto, Canaletto and Van Dyck, collections of Meissen china and exquisite furniture.

There is also an impressive archaeological museum and extensive archive collections, as well as the **Fusiliers of Nothumberland Museum** housed in The Abbot's Tower.

The castle is still the home of the Percys to this day, and is a favourite location for making films, including *Robin Hood Prince of Thieves* and the Harry Potter films, where it doubles as Hogwart's School.

The present Duke and Duchess have transformed the 12 acre gardens creating the impressive **Alnwick Garden** which boasts a superb Grand Cascade enclosed by a Hornbeam Pergola, a scented Rose Garden containing over 2,000 shrub roses and the European inspired Ornamental Garden.

During 2005 further features have been opened including a labyrinth garden, poison garden and the biggest tree house in the country. More features and a new

Tree House, Alnwick Castle Grounds

visitor centre are planned for 2006.

Hulne Park, landscaped by the great Northumbrian born Capability Brown, encompasses the ruins of **Hulne Priory**, the earliest Carmelite Foundation in England dating from 1242.

Alnwick town itself is worthy of an afternoon's exploration with the evocatively named ancient narrow streets of Pottergate, Fenkle Street, Green Batt, Bondgate Without and Bondgate Within. A road leads through the narrow arch of Hotspur Tower, the one surviving part of the town's fortifications, built by the second Duke of Northumberland in the 15th century. All that's left of the once mighty Alnwick Abbey is its 15th century gatehouse, situated just beyond Canongate Bridge.

Each year on Shrove Tuesday the town is host to an annual tradition that begins with the Duke throwing a ball over the castle wall into the town and ends when the ball is retrieved from the river. Traditionally the head of a Scotsman was used, but today the game is played using a more conventional football.

St Michael's Church in Alnwick overlooks the River Aln, and dates from the 15th century. It was unusual in a place as lawless as Northumberland at that time to build a church as large and as splendid as St Michael's.

Alnmouth

The popular and colourful Alnwick Fair, dating from the 13th century, takes place each June.

AROUND ALNWICK

ALNMOUTH

3 miles E of Alnwick off the A1068

Alnmouth is a small seaside resort at the mouth of the River Aln, with fine sandy beaches and two golf courses. The village dates back to the 8th century and was the main sea port for the town of Alnwick in the Middle Ages. John Paul Jones, the Scot who founded the American navy, bombarded the port during the American War of Independence.

The village of Alnmouth is the starting point for many excellent walks along superb stretches of coastline both southwards, past extensive dunes to Warkworth, and north to the former fishing village of Boulmer.

73 THE WIDDRINGTON INN

Widdrington, nr Morpeth

Visitors to the **Widdrington Inn** enjoy traditional hospitality and an exceptional variety of home-cooked dishes.

see page 121

74/132 THE MASONS ARMS

Rennington, nr Alnwick

The **Masons Arms** welcomes visitors with traditional hospitality and well-appointed bedrooms a short drive from the A1.

see pages 121, 141

Beadnell Beach

the Protection of Birds, the island can be visited by boat trips departing from Amble quayside throughout the summer.

AMBLE

7 miles SE of Alnwick on the A1068

Amble is a small port situated at the mouth of the River Coquet, once important for the export of coal, but now enjoying new prosperity as a marina and sea-fishing centre, with a carefully restored harbour. It is a lively place, particularly when the daily catches of fish are being unloaded.

A mile offshore lies **Coquet Island**. It was here that St Cuthbert landed in AD 684. The island's square-towered lighthouse was built in 1841 on the ruins of a 15th century monastery known as Cocwadae. Parts of the monastic building have survived, including a Benedictine cell dating from the 14th century.

Coquet Island had a reputation in former times for causing shipwrecks, but is now a celebrated bird sanctuary, noted for colonies of terns, puffins and eider ducks. Managed by the Royal Society for

BEADNELL

10 miles NE of Alnwick on the B1340

Beadnell is a small fishing village with a harbour and some important 18th-century lime kilns that are now owned by the National Trust. Running eastwards from the harbour into the sea is Ebb's Nook, a narrow strip of land with the scant remains of 13th century **St Ebba's Chapel**, dedicated to the sister of King Oswald, King of Northumbria. This is a delightful stretch of coast, and keen walkers can follow the coastline either by shore path or along the B1340 past St Aidan's Dunes (owned by the National Trust) to Seahouses.

CHATHILL

8 miles N of Alnwick off the A1

Close to Chathill is **Preston Tower**, built by Sir Robert Harbottle, Sheriff of Northumberland, in 1392. The outside walls are seven feet thick, whilst inside are fine tunnel-vaulted rooms which have changed little over the centuries. Two turret rooms have been simply furnished in the style of the period and there are displays depicting the Battle of Flodden and life in the Borders at the start of the 15th century.

CHILLINGHAM

11 miles NW of Alnwick off the B6348

Chillingham is a pleasant estate village best known for the herd of wild, horned white cattle that roam parkland close to Chillingham Castle. Descendants of the cattle that once roamed Britain's forests, they are the only herd of wild white cattle in the country. Chillingham village was built by the Earls of Tankerville and contains many Tudor style houses.

Chillingham Castle is beautifully sited within a 365-acre park. Begun in 1245, the castle belonged for many years to the Grey family who fought many battles with the Scots and the Percy's of Alnwick. Sadly the castle fell into ruin in the 1930s, but was bought in the 1980s by Sir Humphrey Wakefield, a descendant of the Grey family, and has been splendidly restored. Attractions include the impressive Grand Hall, a jousting course, dungeon and torture chamber. The castle and surrounding gardens are open to the public from May to September. Two signposted walks have been laid out through Chillingham Woods, giving superb views over the surrounding countryside.

Just outside Chillingham is the National Trust-owned hill fort Ros Castle, once a vital beacon site visible as far afield as the Scottish hills and Holy Island. The whole area was thrown into chaos in 1804 when an over-

enthusiastic warden lit the beacon by mistake.

CRASTER

6 miles NE of Alnwick off the B1339

Craster is a small, unpretentious fishing village with a reputation for the best oak-smoked kippers in the country. At one time, herring were caught around this coast in vast quantities, but a combination of over-fishing and pollution resulted in a decline in numbers, so the fish now have to be imported. During the kipper curing season, visitors can peer into the smoking sheds where the herring are hung over smouldering piles of oak chips.

South of Craster is **Howick Hall**, built in 1782 and long associated with the Grey family whose family lineage includes many famous public figures – most notably the 2nd Earl Grey, the great social reformer and tea enthusiast. The gardens are open to the public in spring and summer

In recent years Craster and its beautiful coastal surroundings have been used as the location for an ITV comedy-drama called Distant Shores starring Peter Davidson and Samantha Bond. During filming the village was transformed into the island of "Hildasay" and the local pub, The Jolly Fisherman, church, village hall, harbour and other local buildings have all featured in the series.

Craster

and are noted for their beauty, particularly in the rhododendron season.

Craster Quarry was closed in 1939, and is now a small nature reserve called the Arnold Memorial Site. It was this quarry that supplied London and other large cities with its kerbstones. This is the starting point for a pleasant walk along the coastal footpath to Dunstanburgh Castle, or south to Howick, where you will find the site of a Mesolithic house. A reconstruction of the huse stands on the cliffs.

DRURIDGE BAY

12 miles SE of Alnwick off the A1068

Druridge Bay Country Park is set just behind the sand dunes and grasslands of Druridge Bay. The park includes Ladyburn Lake, where there is sailing and windsurfing, plus walking trails, a visitor centre and picnic area. The whole area was once a huge opencast coalmine before it was landscaped and opened as a park in 1989. Nearby are the ruins of medieval Chibburn Preceptory - a small medieval house and chapel that belonged to the Knights Hospitaller.

EDLINGHAM

5 miles SW of Alnwick on the B6341

Edlingham mustn't be confused with the villages of Eglingham and Ellingham, both a few miles to the north. Here at Edlingham the moorland road crosses Corby's Crags, affording visitors one of the finest views in Northumberland. The panorama encompasses the Cheviot Hills in the north, whilst to the south a rolling landscape of heather moors and crags stretches as far as Hadrian's Wall. On a clear day it's possible to catch a glimpse of the high peaks of the North Pennines.

Edlingham Castle was built in the 12th century, but abandoned in 1650 when parts of it collapsed. The ruins were originally thought to be of a simple Northumbrian tower house, but excavations in the late 1970s and early 1980s showed it as having been much more substantial than that.

EGLINGHAM

6 miles NW of Alnwick on the B6346

St Maurice's Church dates from about 1200, and was built on a site granted to the monks of Lindisfarne in AD 738 by King Ceowulf of Northumbria. In 1596 it was attacked by the Scots, and part of the chancel

Castle Ruins, Edlingham

had to be rebuilt in the early 17th century.

A few bumps in a field not far away indicate where the village once stood, and a mile to the southwest is a small hill fort with the quaint name of The Ringses.

ELLINGHAM

7 miles N of Alnwick off the A1

Ellingham is a small agricultural village centred on St Maurice's Church, whose Norman details were all but swept away in a restoration of 1862. It features a central tower instead of the more usual west one. Ellingham Hall stands at the end of a quiet lane beyond the village.

EMBLETON

5 miles NE of Alnwick on the B1339

The dramatic ruins of **Dunstanburgh Castle** stand on a clifftop east of the village, on a site that was originally an Iron Age fort. The fabric of the castle as seen today was built in 1313 by Thomas, Earl of Lancaster, and in the Wars of the Roses it withstood a siege from troops led by Margaret of Anjou, Henry VI's Queen. The damage caused by the siege was never repaired, and the castle remains ruinous to this day.

The castle can't be reached by road, but a path from the village passing through Dunstan Steads, a mile southeast of Embleton, leads to it. The Castle, plus the whole coastline to the north as far as Brunton Burn, is owned by the National Trust.

To the north of Embleton is the village of Newton-by-the-Sea, where there are some attractive 18th century fisherman's cottages built around three sides of a square.

SEAHOUSES

13 miles NE of Alnwick on the B1340

Seahouses is a lively fishing port and small resort with an interesting harbour, magnificent beaches and sand dunes stretching for miles on either side of the town. It is conveniently situated for viewing the Farne Islands, which lie between two and five miles off the coast, and visitors can take a boat trip departing from the harbour to see them at close hand.

WARKWORTH

6 miles S of Alnwick on the A1068

At the southern end of Alnmouth Bay, on the River Coquet, lies **Warkworth Castle**. The site has been fortified since the Iron Age, though the first stone castle was probably built by one 'Roger, son of Richard', who had been granted

75/134 THE PACK HORSE

Ellingham, off A1 8 miles north of Alnwick

The **Pack Horse** is a popular spot for both locals and visitors, with great food and drinks and superior B&B rooms.

🍴 🛏 see pages 121, 142

76/135 THE SCHOONER

North Street, Seahouses

The **Schooner** offers fine hospitality with B&B accommodation.

🍴 🛏 see pages 122, 142

136 ROWENA

Main Street, Seahouses

Rowena welcomes both B&B and self-catering guests on the main street of Seahouses.

🛏 see page 142

Seahouses Harbour

78 DOOLALLY

*Bridge Street,
Berwick-upon-Tweed*

Super seven-day snacks and
an evening menu on Fridays
and Saturdays have quickly
won a following at **Doolally**
café-bistro.

see page 122

the castle by Henry II in the 12th
century.

What can be seen now is
mainly late 12th and 13th century,
including the great Carrickfergus
Tower and the West Postern
Towers, built by Roger's son,
Robert. The castle came into the
ownership of the Percys in 1332
and the family lived here up until
the 16th century. The family crest
can be seen on the Lion Tower.

The most famous of all the
Percy's, Harry (known as Hotspur)
was brought up here.

In 1399 the family created
history for the role they played in
placing Henry Bolingbroke on the
throne as Henry IV. The castle is
now in the care of English
Heritage and is a delightful sight in
spring when the grass mound on
which it stands is covered with
thousands of daffodils. Tel: 01665
711423

An unusual and interesting walk
is signposted to The Hermitage,
along the riverside footpath below
the castle, where a ferry takes you

across the river to visit the tiny
chapel hewn out of solid rock. It
dates from medieval times and was
in use until late in the 16th century.

Warkworth is an interesting and
beautiful village in its own right. An
imposing fortified gatehouse on the
14th century bridge, now only used
by pedestrians, would enable an
invading army to be kept at bay
north of the Coquet. **St
Lawrence's Church** is almost
entirely Norman, though its spire -
an unusual feature on medieval
churches in Northumberland -
dates from the 14th century.

BERWICK-UPON-TWEED

England's northernmost town sits
midway between Edinburgh and
Newcastle. The River Tweed serves
as the border between Scotland and
Northumberland along much of its
length, but a few miles to the west
of Berwick, the border takes a
curious lurch north, and curls up
and over the town to the east
before reaching the coast. So, while
Berwick is on the north bank of
the Tweed, it's well and truly within
Northumberland.

For centuries, this former Royal
burgh of Scotland was fought over
by the Scots and the English, and
changed hands no less than 14
times until it finally became part of
England in 1482. But even now,
Scotland exerts a great influence.
The local football team, Berwick
Rangers, plays in the Scottish
League, and in 1958 the Lord Lyon,

Warkworth Castle

who decides on all matters armorial in Scotland, granted the town a coat-of-arms – the only instance of armorial bearings being granted in Scotland for use in England.

But for many years after becoming English, the town was a curious anomaly. In the 16th century Berwick was declared a free burgh, neither in Scotland nor in England, a situation that lasted right up until 1885. Its ambiguous status was such that when war was declared on Russia in 1853, it was done in the name of "Victoria, Queen of Great Britain, Ireland, Berwick-upon-Tweed and all the British Dominions". When peace was announced in 1856, no mention was made of Berwick. So technically, the town remained at war with Russia.

The situation was rectified in 1966, when a Soviet official made a goodwill visit to the town, and a peace treaty was signed. During the ceremony, the Berwick mayor told the Soviet official that the people of Russia could at last sleep easy in their beds.

Berwick's original medieval walls were built in the 13th century by Edward I. They were subsequently strengthened by Robert the Bruce when he recaptured the town in 1318, and finally rebuilt by Italian engineers at

the bequest of Elizabeth I between 1558 and 1569, though the work was never completed. They are regarded as being the finest preserved fortifications of their time in Europe. The walk around the walls (about 1.5 miles) provides fine views of the town and the Northumberland coastline.

Berwick's strategic location led it to become an important military town. For many years the garrison soldiers were billeted in local taverns and private houses, but this placed a heavy financial burden on the townspeople. Complaints to the government led to the building of Berwick Barracks between 1717 and 1721. Designed by Nicholas Hawksmoor, they were the first purpose-built barracks in Britain, and within them you'll find the **King's Own Scottish Borderers Museum**. Here visitors will learn about a Scottish regiment that was raised in 1689 by the Earl of Leven, and which is still in

77 BONARSTEADS

Northumberland Road, Berwick-upon-Tweed

Bonarsteads is a sociable pub/restaurant with a well-earned strong local following.

¶   see page 122

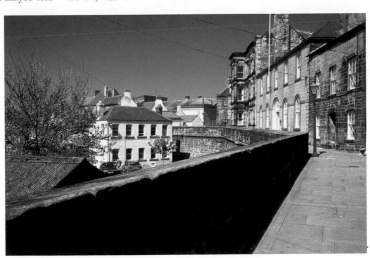

Town Walls, Berwick-upon-Tweed

137 WHYTESIDE HOUSE

*Castlegate,
Berwick-upon-Tweed*

Guests at **Whyteside House** can look forward to a peaceful night's sleep and a super breakfast.

see page 142

138 THE RETREAT & 40 RAVENSDOWNE

*Low Green & Ravensdowne,
Berwick-upon-Tweed*

The Retreat and **40 Ravensdowne** offer a choice of self-catering and B&B accommodation close to the town centre.

see page 143

existence today. Tel: 01289 304493

Housed in the clock tower of the barracks is the **Berwick-upon-Tweed Museum and Art Gallery**, which explores the history of the town. The museum contains a remarkable collection given to the town by Sir William Burrell, who lived in nearby Hutton Castle. Famous for collecting the works of art that can now be seen in the Burrell Art Gallery in Glasgow, Burrell also donated 300 works of art, sculpture and pottery to Berwick. The Gymnasium Gallery, opened in 1993, displays changing exhibitions of contemporary art. Call 01289 301869 for opening times.

Three distinctive bridges linking the town centre with the communities of Tweedmouth and Spittal span the Tweed estuary. The oldest of these is the 17th-century Berwick Bridge, a handsome stone bridge with 15 arches completed in 1626. The Royal Tweed Bridge is the most modern, having been completed in 1928 with a concrete structure built to an iron bridge design. The enormous 126 feet high, 28 arch Royal Border Bridge, carrying the East Coast main-line railway, was built between 1847 and 1850 by Robert Stephenson.

The Berwick skyline is dominated by the imposing Town Hall with its clock tower and steeple that rise to 150 feet, and which is often mistaken for a church. Built between 1754 and 1761, this fine building has a façade as elaborate as its well-documented history. On the ground floor, markets were held in the Exchange and shops and cells existed where now a gift shop and coffee house stand. Guided tours in the summer enable visitors to explore the upper storeys, where there are civic rooms and the former town gaol. A small Cell Block Museum is also located there.

Facing Berwick Barracks is Holy Trinity Church - one of the few Commonwealth churches in England. It was built between 1650 and 1652, during the Commonwealth of Oliver Cromwell, to replace a dilapidated

Royal Tweed Bridge

medieval church, which stood on the same site.

On the northwest side of the town you will find all that remains of **Berwick Castle**. Built in the 13th century, it was demolished in 1850 to make way for the railway station, and the platform now occupies the site of the former Great Hall. The ruins are in the care of English Heritage. The Berwick-upon-Tweed Ramparts comprise gateways, curtain walls and projecting bastions built in 1558 to 1570 to replace earlier defences.

AROUND BERWICK-UPON-TWEED

BAMBURGH

16 miles S of Berwick on the B1340

The seaside village of Bamburgh is dominated by the magnificent **Bamburgh Castle**, epic in scale, even by the standards of this coastline and its abundance of spectacular castles. Situated on a dramatic basalt outcrop on the very edge of the North Sea, it was almost certainly the royal seat of the first kings of Bernicia. The dynasty was founded by the Saxon King Ida in AD 547 and mentioned in the Anglo-Saxon Chronicle. Ida's grandson Ethelfrid united the kingdoms of Bernicia and Deira, and thus created Northumbria, a kingdom that stretched from the Humber to the Forth and was ruled from Bamburgh.

In those days, the castle would have been made of wood – a mighty stockade surrounding a great royal hall, sleeping quarters,

stables, workshops and a garrison for troops. Later on, when Northumbria embraced Christianity, chapels would have been added, and the castle would have been an ostentatious declaration of the Northumbrian kings' power and wealth.

The present stone castle covers eight acres and has an imposing 12th century keep around which three baileys were constructed. The castle was extensively rebuilt and restored in the 18th and 19th centuries, latterly by the first Lord Armstrong whose descendants continue to make this their home.

Bamburgh Castle is open to the public, and rooms on display include

139 ROXBURGH GUEST HOUSE

*Spittall,
nr Berwick-upon-Tweed*

Roxburgh Guest House offers excellent B&B rooms near the beach at Spittall.

⊨ see page 143

140 TWEED VIEW

*East Ord,
nr Berwick-upon-Tweed*

Tweed View is an immaculate B&B on East Ord's village green.

⊨ see page 143

Bamburgh Castle

158 BAMBURGH CASTLE

Bamburgh

Described as one of the finest castles in England, tours are available to see the magnificent interior and its contents.

 see page 153

The village of Bamburgh was the birthplace of Grace Darling, the celebrated Victorian heroine, who in 1838 rowed out with her father from the Longstone Lighthouse in a ferocious storm to rescue the survivors of the steam ship Forfarshire which had foundered on the Farne Islands rocks. She died of tuberculosis only four years later, still only in her twenties, and is buried in the churchyard of St Aidan's. The Grace Darling Museum, in Radcliffe Road, contains memorabilia of the famous rescue.

---

the Armoury, King's Hall, Court Room, Cross Hall, Bakehouse and Victorian Scullery, with collections of tapestries, ceramics, furniture and paintings. Occupying the former laundry room is an exhibition dedicated to the first Lord Armstrong and his many remarkable engineering inventions in the fields of hydraulics, ships, aircraft and arms. Here, too, are relics of aviation in the Bamburgh Castle Aviation Artefacts Museum. Tel: 01668 214515

Just offshore are the **Farne Islands**. This small group of 28 uninhabited islands of volcanic Whin Sill rock provides a major breeding sanctuary for migratory seabirds including puffins, guillemots, razorbills, artic and sandwich terns and kittiwakes. They are the home to a large colony of Atlantic Grey seals, which can often be seen from the beach on the mainland.

The islands have important Christian links, as it was on Inner Farne that St Cuthbert died in AD 687. A little chapel was built here in his memory and restored in Victorian times. The nearby Tower House was built in medieval times by Prior Castell, according to legend, on the site of Cuthbert's cell. Boat trips to the Farne Islands leave from the harbour in Seahouses. Landings are permitted on Inner Farne and Staple Island, times are restricted for conservation reasons and advance booking is necessary at busy times of the year.

BELFORD

14 miles S of Berwick off the A1

Belford is an attractive village of stone houses whose broad main street contains some interesting old shops and a fine old coaching inn, reflecting the fact that this was once an important town on the Great North Road. Today it is an ideal holiday base, standing on the edge of the Kyloe Hills, where there are some fine walks, and close to the long golden beaches and rocky outcrops of the coast.

St Cuthbert's Cave, to the north of Belford, is only accessible by foot. It is completely natural, and concealed by a great overhanging rock surrounded by woodland. It is believed that the saint's body lay here on its much interrupted journey across Northumbria. From the summit of nearby Greensheen Hill there are superb views of the coast and of the Cheviots to the west.

DUDDO

7 miles SW of Berwick on the B6354

Close to the village are the **Duddo Stones**, one of Northumberland's most important ancient monuments. This ancient stone circle, which now consists of five upright stones over seven feet high, dates back to around 2000 BC, and can only be reached from the village by foot.

HORNCLIFFE

4 miles W of Berwick off the A698

The village of Horncliffe, five miles upstream of Berwick, can only be reached by one road that leads into and out of the village, making it feel rather remote. Many visitors are unaware of the existence of the river, but there is nothing more pleasant than wandering down one of the paths leading to the banks to watch the salmon fishermen on a summer's evening.

Not far from Horncliffe, the River Tweed is spanned by the Union Suspension Bridge linking Scotland and England, built in 1820 by Sir Samuel Browne, who also invented the wrought-iron chain links used in its construction. The graceful structure, 480 feet long, was Britain's first major suspension bridge to carry vehicular traffic, and although not carrying a major road, it is still possible to drive over it.

LINDISFARNE, OR HOLY ISLAND

10 miles S of Berwick off the A1

Northumberland's northern coastline is dominated by Holy Island, also known by its Celtic name of Lindisfarne. The island is accessible only at low tide, via a 3 mile-long causeway linking it with the mainland at Beal. Tide tables are published locally and are displayed at each end of the road. There are refuges part ways along for those who fail to time it correctly.

As you cross, note the 11th-century Pilgrims' Way, marked by stakes, still visible about 200 metres south of the modern causeway. This route was in use until comparatively recent times.

The island was given to St Aidan in AD 635 by Oswald, King of Northumbria. St Aidan and his small community of Irish monks came from Iona to found a base from which to convert northern England to Christianity. This led to the island being called one of the cradles of English Christianity. St Cuthbert came here to teach and the island became a magnet for pilgrims. When he died in AD 687

79 APPLE INN

Lucker, nr Belford

Traditional charm, real ales and home cooking await both visitors and locals at the **Apple Inn**.

🍴 *see page 123*

159 LINDISFARNE PRIORY

Lindisfarne

Across the causeway on Holy Island, Lindisfarne Priory is one of the Holiest sites in England. The museum depicts life as it was over a millenium ago.

🏛 *see page 154*

Lindisfarne

**80/141   THE WHITE
                 SWAN**

Lowick, nr Berwick-upon-Tweed

A short diversion from the A1 rewards visitors to the **White Swan** with a great choice of excellent home cooking and two rooms for B&B.

see pages 123, 143

Holy Island village is a community of around 170 people who work mainly in farming and the tourist trade. Some are also employed in the island's distillery, noted for excellent traditional mead, which can be purchased locally. Much of the island is also a nature reserve, with wildflowers and a wide variety of seabirds. St Mary's Church in the village has some fine Saxon stonework above the chancel arch.

---

he was buried in the church. St Cuthbert's island can be reached at low tide from the island and was used by the saint during times of solitude. A cross marks the site of his tiny chapel.

The early monks are remembered for producing some of the finest surviving examples of Celtic art - the richly decorated Lindisfarne Gospels, dating from the 7th century. When the island was invaded by Vikings in the 9th century, the monks fled taking their precious gospels with them. These have, miraculously, survived and are now in the safety of the British Museum. Facsimiles are kept on Lindisfarne and can be seen in the 12th century parish church on the island. The monks also took with them St Cuthbert's bones and wandered around for over 100 years with them before eventually finding a safe resting place in Durham.

During the 11th century a group of Benedictine monks settled here, and the ruins of their great sandstone **Lindisfarne Priory** with its Romanesque great pillars can still be explored.

Lindisfarne Castle was established in Tudor times as yet another fortification to protect the exposed flank of Northumbria from invasion by the Scots. In 1902 it was bought by Edward Hudson, the owner of *Country Life* magazine, who employed the great Edwardian architect Sir Edward Lutyens to rebuild and restore it as a private house. It is now in the care of the

National Trust, and the house and its small walled garden are open to the public during the summer months. Tel: 01289 389244

The island is the finishing point for the 62-mile long **St Cuthbert's Way**, a long distance footpath which opened in 1996. The trail begins at Melrose, across the Scottish border, and along the way passes through the Northumberland National Park and the Cheviot Hills.

LOWICK

8 miles S of Berwick on the B6353

Lowick is a quiet farming community which contains only a few shops and a couple of pubs. About a mile east of the village are the earthworks of a former castle. The Norman church was replaced by the present St John the Baptist Church.

NORHAM

6 miles SW of Berwick on the B6470

Norham is a neat village on the banks of the Tweed. Up until 1836 the town was an enclave of the County Palatine of Durham, surrounded by Northumberland on the south, east and west, and Scotland on the north. **Norham Castle** was built in the 12th century by the Bishop of Durham on a site of great natural strength, guarding a natural ford over the river. It withstood repeated attacks in the 13th and 14th centuries and was thought to be impregnable. However, in 1513 it was stormed by the forces of James IV on his way to Flodden and partially destroyed.

Although it was later rebuilt, the castle was again destroyed by the Scots in 1530, and had lost its importance as a defensive stronghold by the end of the 16th century. The castle is now under the care of English Heritage. Tel: 01289 382329

Norham's Station Museum is located on the former Tweedmouth-Kelso branch line. The museum features the original signal box, booking office, porter's room model railway. Tel: 01289 382217

Church of St John the Baptist, Lowick

TILLMOUTH

9 miles SW of Berwick on the A698

The village of Tillmouth lies along the banks of the River Till, a tributary of the Tweed which is crossed by the 15th-century Twizel Bridge, although a more modern structure now carries the A698 over the river. Up until the building of the 1727 Causey Arch in County Durham, the old Twizel Bridge, with a span of 90 feet, had the largest span of any bridge in Britain. There are some lovely walks here and a well-signed footpath leads to the ruins of Twizel Castle, and the remains of St Cuthbert's Chapel on the opposite bank, dating from the 18th or 19th centuries, but incorporating some medieval stonework.

TWEEDMOUTH

1 mile S of Berwick off the A1

Tweedmouth and Spittal, on the English side of the Tweed estuary, are largely suburbs of Berwick. In mid-July a ceremony is held in Tweedmouth, dating back to 1292, to celebrate the fact that the River Tweed, one of the best salmon rivers in Britain, reaches the sea here. The local schools hold a ballot to elect a Salmon Queen, and her crowning marks the beginning of Feast Week which centres on a church service and involves lots of festivities including a traditional salmon supper.

WAREN MILL

15 miles SE of Berwick on the B1342

Waren Mill is a small village situated on Budle Bay, a large inlet of flats and sand where vast numbers of wading birds and wildfowl come to feed. Caution should be taken when walking on the flats, as sections quickly become cut off at high tide.

Each year in Norham an unusual ceremony takes place. The Blessing of the Nets is held at midnight on 13th February to mark the beginning of the salmon fishing season. The service is held by lantern light, with the clergyman standing in a boat in the middle of the river.

81/142 THE ROB ROY RESTAURANT WITH ROOMS

Dock Road, Tweedmouth

The **Rob Roy** has won countless friends with its superb food and smart bedrooms.

see pages 123, 143

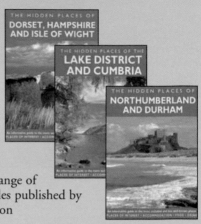

Advertisements

Food and Drink in Northumbria

The selection of establishments serving food and drink featured in this section includes restaurants, cafés, hotels, pubs, inns and tea & coffee shops. Each establishment has an entry number which is used to identify its location on the map below and its name and short address in the list below the map. The entry number can also be used to find more information and contact details for the establishment in the ensuing pages. In addition full details of establishments serving food and drink featured in this section may be found on the Travel Publishing website – www.travelpublishing.co.uk This website has a large database of establishments serving food and drink covering the whole of Britain and Ireland.

FOOD AND DRINK

1	The Garden House, Durham	41	The Bay Horse Hotel, Wolsingham
2	Tut 'n' Shive, Bishop Aukland	42	Simonburn Tea Rooms and B&B, Simonburn
3	Stonebridge Inn, Neville's Cross	43	The Hadrian Hotel, Wall
4	The Bay Horse Inn, Brandon Village	44	The Royal Hotel, Priestpopple
5	The Ship Inn, High Hesleden	45	The County Hotel, Priestpopple
6	The Royal George, Old Shotton Village	46	The Sun Inn, Acomb
7	The Wayfarers Inn, Haswell	47	The Rose & Crown, Slaley
8	The Red Lion, Trimdon Village	48	Dyvels Hotel, Corbridge
9	The Fir Tree, Wingate	49	The Golden Lion, Corbridge
10	The George, Darlington	50	Barrasford Arms Hotel, Barrasford
11	The Otter & Fish, Hurworth-on-Tees	51	The Railway Hotel, Haydon Bridge
12	Lord Nelson, Gainford	52	Hadrians Lodge Hotel, Haydon Bridge
13	Pathfinders, Maltby	53	Old Repeater Station, Grindon
14	The Bay Horse , Middridge	54	The Golden Lion, Allendale
15	The Vane Arms, Thorpe Thewles	55	Allendale Tea Rooms, Allendale
16	The Sutton Arms, Faceby	56	The Milecastle Inn, Cawfields
17	The Half Moon, Lazenby	57	The Otterburn Tower Hotel, Otterburn
18	Zetland Hotel, Marske-by-the-Sea	58	Elm Tree Coffee Shop, Rothbury
19	Mars Inn, Loftus	59	The Turks Head, Rothbury
20	Bradleys Tea & Coffee Shop, Consett	60	Ryecroft Hotel, Wooler
21	The Crown & Crossed Swords, Shotley Bridge	61	The Collingwood Arms, Cornhill-on-Tweed
22	The Royal Oak, Medomsley	62	The Anglers Arms, Weldon Bridge
23	The Jolly Drover, Leadgate	63	Embleton Hall, Longframlington
24	The Derwent Walk Inn, Ebchester	64	The New Inn, Longframlington
25	Chez Neil's, Oxhill	65	Black Bull, Etal Village
26	Cronniwell Village Inn, Hamsterley	66	The Fox & Hounds, Wylam
27	The Coach & Horses, Leyburn Hold	67	The Jiggery Pokery, Mickley Square
28	Penny's Tea Rooms, Barnard Castle	68	The Rising Sun, Crawcrook
29	The Country Style Bakery & Tea Rooms, Middleton-in-Teesdale	69	The Anglers Arms, Choppington
		70	The Fleece Inn, Bondgate Without
30	The Bowes Incline Hotel, Birtley	71	Narrowgate Restaurant, Narrowgate
31	The Raby Arms Hotel, Barnard Castle	72	The Oddfellows Arms, Narrowgate
32	High Force Hotel, Forest-in-Teesdale	73	The Widdrington Inn, Widdrington
33	The Red Lion Hotel, Cotherstone	74	The Masons Arms, Rennington
34	The Rose & Crown, Mickleton	75	The Pack Horse, Ellingham
35	Teesdale Hotel, Middleton-in-Teesdale	76	The Schooner, Seahouses
36	The Strathmore Arms, Holwick	77	Bonarsteads, Berwick-upon-Tweed
37	The White Monk Tearoom, Blanchland	78	Doolally, Berwick-upon-Tweed
38	The Rookhope Inn, Rookhope	79	Apple Inn, Lucker
39	The Cross Keys Inn, Eastgate	80	The White Swan, Lowick
40	The Railway Inn, Fourstones	81	The Rob Roy Restaurant with Rooms, Tweedmouth

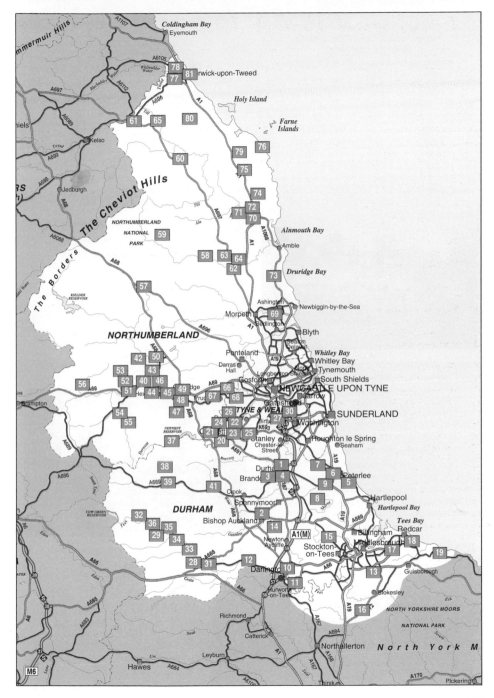

1 THE GARDEN HOUSE

North Road, Durham DH1 4NQ
☎ 0191 384 3460
e-mail: gardenhousedurham@aol.com

Paul Mash brought a wealth of experience in the licensed trade when he took over the **Garden House** with his family at the beginning of 2005. Close to the city centre and an easy walk to the Cathedral, this attractively modernised coaching house serves a good selection of beers and lagers, bar snacks, and a full menu in the conservatory restaurant. The Garden House also has five smart en suite bedrooms for guests spending time exploring Durham's many places of interest.

2 TUT 'N' SHIVE

Newgate Street, Bishop Auckland,
Co Durham DL14 7EQ
☎ 01388 603252

The **Tut 'n' Shive** is a convivial town pub with super friendly staff. The changing selection of real ales is supplemented by lagers and ciders. Great value lunches. Live music at weekends.

Explore Britain and Ireland with *Hidden Places* guides - a fascinating series of national and local travel guides.

www.travelpublishing.co.uk

0118-981-7777

info@travelpublishing.co.uk

3 STONEBRIDGE INN

Stonebridge, Neville's Cross,
Durham DH1 3RX
☎ 0191 386 9591

By the A690 on the western outskirts of the city, the **Stonebridge Inn** has a fine reputation for high-quality cooking matched by value for money and excellent service. It started life in the 1860s as a coaching inn, and the interior has retained a lovely traditional look assisted by beams and old oak floorboards, and outside is a pleasant little patio that's popular in the summer.

Food is served every day from 11 o'clock to 9 and runs the gamut from ciabattas and jacket potatoes to salads, meat and fish dishes (the fish arrives fresh every day) and always a good choice for vegetarians.

The inn is also a much-loved 'local', with a hardworking host in Graham Baldridge; pool and darts are played in a separate part of the bar, and thirsts are quenched with a choice of real ales.

4 THE BAY HORSE INN

Brandon Village, nr Durham DH7 8ST
☎ 0191 378 0498

Clair and Peter are the new owners of the **Bay Horse Inn**, an attractive hostelry on a corner site near the A690 southwest of Durham City. It's a fine base for exploring the sights of Durham and the surrounding area, and the 10 modern en suite guest rooms include a family room sleeping up to four.

The rooms are in a single-storey building at the back of the hotel, with disabled access and parking right outside. Clair and Peter have the services of a talented chef who gets his meat from a top local butcher and other supplies from the best local sources. The restaurant is open for lunch and dinner every day, and the accomplished cooking is matched by very good service and excellent value for money.

5 THE SHIP INN

**Main Street, High Hesleden,
nr Hartlepool TS27 4QD**
☎ 01429 836453 Fax: 01429 836453

Diners and drinkers come from all over the region to **The Ship Inn**, a splendid, spacious free house on the B1281, just off the A19 and close to the Castle Eden Dene National Nature Reserve. The pub's name is reflected in the décor, which includes models of sailing ships (one is even suspended over the bar), and there are views of the sea and boats from the beer garden and car park.

The pub's reputation for real ale is richly deserved, with five or six brews always on

tap, but the food is held in equally high esteem by all who know this place. Sheila Crosby, who runs the pub with her husband Peter, is a terrific cook, and her lengthy menus and daily specials offer a choice that is second to none. Black pudding and haggis medley with colcannon and pepper sauce is a well-loved Ship Inn favourite, and the blackboard specials could include such delights as sea bass with toasted scallops, or chargrilled chicken with coriander pesto. The Ship is open from 6 every day, also from 12 to 2.30 Friday to Sunday.

6 THE ROYAL GEORGE

**Old Shotton Village, nr Peterlee,
Co Durham SR8 2ND
☎ 0191 587 0526**

The **Royal George** is kept as neat as a new pin by the Slee family. In the homely public bar and lounge/dining area draught beers and ciders are dispensed from 11.30, and well-priced food is served.

7 THE WAYFARERS INN

**78 Front Street East, Haswell,
Co Durham DH6 2BL
☎ 0191 526 2111**

Andrew and Laura run the **Wayfarers Inn**, a convivial pub on a corner site in Haswell. Home cooking covers the range of classic English dishes. Closed Tuesday.

8 THE RED LION

**Front Street North, Trimdon Village,
Co Durham TS29 6PG ☎ 01429 880274**

In a pretty village hidden away in the Durham countryside but easily reached from the A19, the **Red Lion** is maintained in pristine order inside and out by proprietors Gordon and Sheila Wright. They also keep their ales in tip-top condition, and the home cooking brings hungry visitors from near and far. Typical main dishes (the choice changes daily) include paupiette of haddock and smoked salmon, duck with ginger, redcurrants and red onion marmalade, and braised lamb shanks.

9 THE FIR TREE

**Durham Road, Wingate,
Co Durham TS28 5HS
☎ 01429 837135**

Gary and Julie Noble keep out the welcome mat at the **Fir Tree**, an imposing pub located at a busy crossroads close to the A19. The couple have transformed the interior, renewing the carpets and furniture and generally creating a smart, comfortable ambience while retaining the traditional feel.

Long popular with the locals, the Fir Tree also attracts motorists and tourists with its winning combination of friendly atmosphere, real ales and home cooking. The renowned steak pie is just one of a long list of main courses, and booking is essential for the super Sunday lunch. Food is served Tues 5pm-9pm, Wed-Sat 12-2pm & 5pm-9pm, Sun 12-3pm. The pub itself opens during normal pub opening hours.

100

10 THE GEORGE

Bondgate, Darlington DL3 7LB
☎ 01325 481686

David Nicholls woos the locals with a fine selection of real ales and good unpretentious food at the **George**, where he has been the host since 1998. Sandwiched among shops in the town centre, it has been a Darlington landmark since 1837, and remains a popular, no-nonsense all-day venue for a drink. Food is served from 11 to 3 Monday to Saturday. The George also has four well-priced rooms for B&B.

11 THE OTTER & FISH

The Street, Hurworth-on-Tees,
nr Darlington DL2 2AH
☎ 01325 720019

Close to the Yorkshire border, the **Otter & Fish** stands opposite the river in Hurworth. Recently refurbished, it is open lunchtime and evening and all day Sunday for drinks and home-cooked food.

12 LORD NELSON

Main Road, Gainford, nr Darlington,
Co Durham DL2 3DY ☎ 01325 730381
e-mail: lord-nelson@supanet.com

Recent renovation by Punch Taverns has added to the already considerable appeal of the **Lord Nelson**, which stands on the A67 in a pretty village on the River Tees. The stonework has been restored to its former splendid state, and the décor in the public areas has been smartly modernised. The bar and toilets are wheelchair-accessible. A selection of cask ales, beers and lagers can be enjoyed on their own or to accompany bar snacks and traditional English dishes served lunchtime and evening every day.

13 PATHFINDERS

High Lane, Maltby,
nr Stockton-on-Tees TS8 0BY
☎ 01642 590300
e-mail: pathfinderinn@aol.com

Landlady Georgette Snaith is the driving force behind **Pathfinders**, a charming pub in a quiet little village close to the A19 south of Stockton and Middlesbrough. Drinks, including several well-kept ales, are served from 11 o'clock, and every lunchtime and evening a fine selection of home-cooked dishes is

listed on the menu. Tried and tested classics are to the fore, including garlic prawns or mussels, traditional fish & chips, steak & ale pie and sausage & mash in a giant Yorkshire pudding.

14 THE BAY HORSE

Middridge, nr Newton Aycliffe,
Co Durham DL5 7JD
☎ 01325 312653

At the beginning of 2005 business partners Amanda Richardson and John Burdiss took over the **Bay Horse**, which reverted to its first name after years when it known as the Poachers Pocket. The original Bay Horse dates back to the middle of the 18th century, and it has undergone many changes down the years. The interior is a place of many moods, and the large floor space is an appealing blend of old and new, with handsome

panelling, beams, a mix of darkwood and lightwood furniture, and a number of cosy little corners in which to enjoy a drink.

The newly completed restaurant is contrastingly light and airy, an appropriate setting in a venue where the cooking is definitely king. The menu changes constantly, providing a fine choice that caters for all tastes and appetites. The sizzling platters have quickly won the approval of the many regular customers, who return time after time for Szechuan beef or chicken and Singapore steak, chicken and king prawns. Chicken with black bean sauce is another exotic favourite, while more traditional palates are equally well catered for with such dishes as Barnsley chops, fisherman's pie, steak & mushroom suet pudding, lamb hotpot and a super liver & sausage casserole.

An upstairs suite is available for functions and special occasions, and the Bay Horse has an excellent beer garden and ample parking. It stands two miles southeast of Bishop Auckland between Shildon and Aycliffe, and is easily reached from either the A167 or the A6072. Well worth a visit in its own right for either a drink or a meal, the Bay Horse also provides a very pleasant break for business people, motorists or tourists discovering the sights of the area: among these are the National Railway Museum at Shildon and the castle and St Andrew's Church in Bishop Auckland.

15 THE VANE ARMS

Thorpe Thewles,
Stockton-on-Tees TS21 3JU
☎ 01740 630458
e-mail: thevanearms@btinternet.com

South of Sedgefield on the A177 Stockton road the **Vane Arms**, built in the 17th century, overlooks the green in the pretty village of Thorpe Thewles. Gordon McPhail has made many improvements to the décor in the bar, and attractive pictures line the walls of the restaurant. The Chef is a dab hand at classic English cooking, with steaks, cottage pie and seafood

specials among the favourites. Food is served every session except Sunday and Monday evenings.

16 THE SUTTON ARMS

Faceby, nr Middlesbrough TS9 7BW
☎ 01642 700382

Built in the 18th century and rebuilt at the beginning of the 20th, the **Sutton Arms** once again presents a pristine face to the world after a major refurbishment programme by Yvonne and Dave Lee. This handsome roadside inn at the top of the North York Moors National Park has a delightful little bar with low beams and sturdy iron-based tables, and an elegant restaurant. Black Sheep heads the list of cask ales, and the home-cooked dishes include a super steak pie and traditional Sunday lunch (no food Monday).

17 THE HALF MOON

High Street, Lazenby,
nr Middlesbrough TS6 8DX
☎ 01642 452752 Fax: 01642 453527

In the village of Lazenby, just off the A174 east of Middlesbrough, the **Half Moon** has rightly earned its reputation as 'a great place to eat, drink and enjoy'.

Built in the 1900s and rebuilt a century later, it presents an attractive face to the world with a colourful collection of flowers and shrubs, and a backdrop of distant trees can be seen from the terrace.

Inside, Jill Palmer and Paul Kidney have created a particularly cosy, friendly atmosphere, and the traditional bar is a splendid spot for a chat and a drink – Timothy Taylor Landlord, Black Sheep and Old Speckled hen are among the favourite brews. Food is a big part of the Half Moon's business, with a menu of home-style snacks and

dishes served all day. The choice runs from a baguette sandwich with an interesting filling such as lemon pepper

chicken or bacon & black pudding to main courses typified by pork, apple & cider pie, liver & onions or Cajun chicken. Ramp access to the bar and wheelchair access to the toilets. No smoking throughout.

18 ZETLAND HOTEL

9 High Street, Marske-by-the-Sea,
Tees Valley TS11 6JQ
☎ 01642 483973
e-mail: annallsopp@btconnect.co.uk

Ann Allsopp has a friendly greeting for
everyone at the **Zetland Hotel**, which stands
in the centre of Marske-by-the-Sea, just down
the coast from Redcar. Open every day from
11, this handsome 19th century hotel has
public and lounge bars and a pretty restaurant
serving generous portions of unpretentious
dishes. The coast and countryside have plenty
to offer, and the Zetland provides a very
pleasant base with six comfortable bedrooms.

19 MARS INN

Deepdale Road, Loftus,
Tees Valley TS13 4RS
☎ 01287 642993 Fax: 01287 642993

The **Mars Inn** presents a leafy face to the
world with its coat of
trees and shrubs. The
spacious bar-lounge is
open all day for drinks
(Black Sheep and guest
ales), snacks and light
dishes.

20 BRADLEYS TEA & COFFEE SHOP

18a Middle Street, Consett, Co Durham
☎ 01207 581519

Townspeople, shoppers and visitors enjoy
good traditional homemade meals and snacks
served at **Bradleys
Tea & Coffee Shop**.
On the first floor of
a modern shopping
block, Bradleys is
open all day Monday
to Saturday.

21 THE CROWN & CROSSED SWORDS

Shotley Bridge, nr Consett,
Co Durham DH8 0HU
☎ 01207 502006

Shotley
Bridge is
the place
where
steel-
making
started in
this
region. It
became a
spa town,
and its
prosperity
has a

legacy in many fine houses that survive. One
of them, originally a swordmaking warehouse,
is now the **Crown & Crossed Swords**, near
the A68 and a short distance from
Consett. Run by the same family for 50
years, the pub has a delightful traditional
bar, an upstairs restaurant and 10 good-
sized bedrooms for B&B guests.

22 THE ROYAL OAK

7 Manor Road, Medomsley, nr Consett,
Co Durham DH8 6QN
☎ 01207 560336 Fax: 01207 560336
e-mail: michaellivermore@hotmail.com

Set back from the road in a village close to
Consett and Shotley Bridge, the **Royal Oak**
is a handsome stone building dating from the
late-18th century. Hardworking host Michael
Livermore is overseeing a major
refurbishment programme and is aiming to
widen the appeal of what has long been a
popular locals pub. One of his main
ambitions is to make this splendid old pub a
destination restaurant serving food of
worldwide inspiration.

23 THE JOLLY DROVER

**Redwell Hill, Leadgate, nr Consett,
Co Durham DH8 6RR
☎ 01207 503994**

The **Jolly Drover** dates from the 17th century and is tastefully modernised. Inside, there's plenty of space, including several dining areas, for enjoying a drink and good honest pub dishes.

24 THE DERWENT WALK INN

**Ebchester Hill, Ebchester,
Co Durham DH8 0SX
☎ 01207 560347 Fax: 01207 560347**

The **Derwent Walk Inn** is a friendly pub with super views of the Derwent Valley. Visitors can look forward to a good choice of real ales and wines, and an extensive menu served all day.

25 CHEZ NEIL'S

**The Ox Inn, Oxhill, Stanley, Co Durham
☎ 01207 290888**

The Neil of **Chez Neil's** is Neil Timby, an accomplished chef who has the food franchise here at the Ox Inn. Neil's passion for food has won many friends in this part of Co Durham, and in the 46-cover restaurant he offers a winning combination of fine cooking and great value for money. Classic English stalwarts include

battered cod, toad-in-the-hole, homemade corned beef & potato pie, sausage, liver & bacon casserole and the day's roast (four roasts for Sunday lunch). More exotic options might include Thai salmon or beef in black bean sauce. Blackboard specials extend the choice still further.

26 CRONNIWELL VILLAGE INN

**Victoria Terrace, Hamsterley,
nr Newcastle NE17 7SH
☎ 01207 561992 Fax: 01207 560719**

Keith and Lynda Telford have recently taken over the **Cronniwell Village Inn** from Lynda's mother, so the family connection remains strong. Always a favourite with the locals, the inn also attracts a considerable passing trade, as it stands on the A694 road that links Consett with Newcastle-upon-Tyne.

The inn has had several incarnations in its life, and the pretty village pub of today has been tastefully modernised while retaining a delightful traditional appeal, and prints and pictures in the public rooms depict the area in former days. Keith and Lynda started to serve food in July 2005, and a free supper accompanies the Sunday night quiz. The inn also provides a convenient base for motorists, whether on business or leisure travel, and there are plans to add to the 5 bedrooms currently available.

27 THE COACH & HORSES

**Leyburn Hold, Birtley,
Tyne & Wear DH3 1QF
☎ 0191 492 3999**

Colin Pearson and his family took over the **Coach & Horses** at the beginning of 2005, bringing many years' experience in the pub trade. On the old A1 at the top of town, the pub dates from the 1930s, and behind the small-paned windows there's a traditional look in the bar and lounge. Colin is a talented

self-taught chef, and in the new 40-cover restaurant diners can choose from a wide selection of good-value dishes to suit all tastes. The Coach & Horses is very family-friendly, and the garden has swings and a slide.

28 PENNY'S TEA ROOMS

**Market Place, Barnard Castle, Co Durham
☎ 01833 637634**

Penny's has recently added overnight accommodation to its established role as a popular all-day tea room and licensed restaurant. Traditional home-made food. Open Tue-Sat 9-5, Sun 10-5, also Bank Holidays.

29 THE COUNTRY STYLE BAKERY & TEA ROOMS

**Market Place, Middleton-in-Teesdale,
Co Durham DL12 0QS
☎ 01833 640924**

The Country Style Bakery & Tea Rooms is a great place for enjoying sandwiches, hot and cold snacks, pies, pastries, gluten free cakes and super cream teas.

30 THE BOWES INCLINE HOTEL

**Northside, Birtley, Co Durham DH3 1RF
☎ 0191 410 4756
⊕ www.bowesinclinehotel.co.uk**

The **Bowes Incline** is a hotel, pub and restaurant in a beautiful setting with magnificent views across the rolling countryside. It lies just off the A1 within a short walk of the amazing Angel of the North, and is equally

appealing as a place to pause on a journey, a destination restaurant and a base for both tourists and business people.

The hotel, run by Douglas Rowe and his family, has 15 guest bedrooms (including a family room), all with bath and shower en suite, hairdryer, tea/coffee tray, television and telephone with modem socket. The rooms are on a single level, and one is specially adapted for disabled guests. Top of the range is a room whose ceiling glows at night with a depiction of the moon and the stars. The Bowes Bar is a pleasant place to meet for a drink or an informal meal, and Sisters Restaurant offers an à la carte menu and a list of daily specials; a pianist plays on Saturday evenings. The restaurant can be used for functions, and conference rooms cater for up to 150 delegates.

31 THE RABY ARMS HOTEL

Market Place, Barnard Castle,
Co Durham DL12 8NF
☎ 01833 695035

Close to the shops and a short walk from the spectacular Bowes Museum, the **Raby Arms** has long been a landmark on Barnard Castle's market place. Originally a hotel, it is now a popular pub and restaurant, pleasantly modernised while retaining a good deal of period appeal. Hosts David and Sharon have a warm welcome for all their visitors, and amenities include baby-changing facilities and a wheelchair-accessible toilet.

Sharon is in charge of the stoves, and her wide-ranging menu caters for all tastes and appetites; popular dishes include sausages and steaks from an excellent local butcher, and cod from Whitby served in large or smaller sizes. There are dining areas on the ground and first floors, and an upstairs room can be booked for private parties and functions. The Raby Arms is also a popular place to meet for a drink, and when the weather is kind the rear patio is a popular spot.

32 HIGH FORCE HOTEL

Forest-in-Teesdale, nr Barnard Castle,
Co Durham DL12 0XH
☎ 01833 622222
e-mail: mickclegg@btinternet.com
🌐 www.highforcehotel.com

Michael and Vicky Clegg have been at the helm of the famous **High Force Hotel** since 2003, and the improvements they have made in all areas have enhanced its reputation as one of the finest in the region. It was originally a hunting lodge, with royalty among its patrons, and photographs in the bar recall a visit by the future King Edward VII. The day rooms have a very comfortable,

traditional appeal, and the immaculate bedrooms, all with full en suite facilities, guarantee a peaceful night's sleep.

The day starts with an excellent breakfast, and every lunchtime and evening Vicky and her team prepare a fine selection of bar and restaurant meals. Mick's speciality is their own recipe and award winning High Force cask ales, Cauldron Snout and Forest XB. Just minutes from the hotel there are wonderful walks along the banks of the Tees, but the main local attraction is the one that gives the hotel its name – the spectacular waterfall that is one of the wonders of the English landscape.

33 THE RED LION HOTEL

Cotherstone, nr Barnard Castle,
Co Durham DL12 9QE
☎ 01833 650236
e-mail: theredlion@comtech.uk.net

Lovers of traditional village pubs appreciate the qualities of the **Red Lion Hotel**, which has remained virtually unchanged in appearance for more than 250 years. The cosy interior features rich-red appointments and an

open fire, creating an ambience that attracts both locals and visitors. A selection of Cask Marque

approved real ales is on tap in the bar, and food is served on weekend evenings in the non-smoking restaurant. Host Richard Robinson has a friendly greeting for all-comers, including children, dogs – even walkers in muddy boots! Pub hours are 7 to 11, also Saturday lunchtime.

34 THE ROSE & CROWN

Mickleton, nr Middleton-in-Teesdale,
Co Durham
☎ 01833 640381

The **Rose & Crown** is a handsome greystone building standing on the B6281 between Romaldkirk and Middleton-in-Teesdale. It's a great base for a sporting, walking or touring holiday, and the three guest bedrooms all have washbasins, television and tea/coffee tray. At the back of the pub is a large caravan park looking out over open countryside. The Rose & Crown is popular with locals and motorists, with pleasant bars and a dining area serving rotating real ales and traditional English dishes.

35 TEESDALE HOTEL

Market Square, Middleton-in-Teesdale, nr
Barnard Castle, Co Durham DL12 0QG
☎ 01833 640264
e-mail: john@falconer0.wanadoo.co.uk
🌐 www.teesdalehotel.com

Guests return year after year to the **Teesdale Hotel**, which started life as a coaching house in the 17th century. Hospitality is in generous supply here, and the lounge bar is a warm, comfortable and convivial place where guests and non-residents are equally welcome, and residents also have their own lounge for relaxing after the day's activities or planning the next day's trips. The 14 well-appointed

bedrooms include singles, twins, doubles and a family room, and all have en suite facilities.

The hotel also offers a wide choice of bar and restaurant meals and is also a pleasant spot for morning coffee or afternoon tea. Middleton-in-Teesdale, the capital of Upper Teesdale, enjoys a superb setting, in the market place surrounded by green hills. It is an ideal centre for a walking holiday or for exploring both Teesdale and the entire North Pennines; among the many nearby attractions are High Force, England's largest waterfall, Cauldron Snout, England's largest cascade, other dramatic falls and several historic castles.

36 THE STRATHMORE ARMS

Holwick, nr Middleton-in-Teesdale,
Co Durham DL12 0NJ
☎ 01833 640362
🖥 www.strathmore20atbtbusiness.co.uk

The **Strathmore Arms** is a traditional country pub in a superb setting close to the River Tees. Coal fires blaze a welcome in the classic bar and dining area, where real ales and hearty home-cooked food keep visitors happy (connoisseurs of real ale head here for the beer festivals held three times a year). With 4 en suite bedrooms, the inn is a perfect base for a

walking holiday: the Pennine Way runs close by, and a wealth of scenic attractions includes the spectacular High Force waterfall. Adjacent to the inn is a campsite with toilet and washing facilities.

37 THE WHITE MONK TEAROOM

The Old School, Blanchland,
County Durham DH8 9ST
☎ 01434 675044

A quintessentially English tearoom, located right in the heart of the medieval village of Blanchland, **The White Monk Tearoom** is housed in the Old School built in 1855 and named after the French monks who once wore white habits. The Old School is a prominent and attractive building tastefully decorated and furnished with a delightful walled garden at the rear to sit in and have coffee on a pleasant summers day. This is a traditional English Tearoom serving afternoon teas, freshly made sandwiches, scones, cakes and biscuits, all homemade including the famous homemade Rhubarb Jam. Open Easter to End of October, 7 days a week 10.30am to 5pm. Winter Sat & Sun 10.30am to 5pm

38 THE ROOKHOPE INN

Rookhope, Weardale,
Co Durham DL13 2BD
☎ 01388 517215 Fax: 01388 517861
e-mail: chris@rookhope.com
🖥 www.rookhope.com

Chris Joncs has made a fine job of restoring the **Rookhope Inn** to its status as both a convivial village local and a place to seek out for food and accommodation. Real ales from Jennings Cockermouth Brewery and a fine selection of wines and malts are served in the bar, and

classic English dishes offer excellent value for money; freshly cut sandwiches provide a lighter alternative at lunchtime. Very much the hub of village life, the inn has a games room and regularly hosts live music evenings. For overnight guests there are five well-appointed bedrooms. Dogs are very welcome.

39 THE CROSS KEYS INN

Eastgate, nr Stanhope, Weardale,
Co Durham
☎ 01388 517234

Tourists, walkers and cyclists join the locals at the **Cross Keys Inn**, where the new tenants provide a warm, genuine welcome. Home-cooked food, 2 B&B rooms.

40 THE RAILWAY INN

Fourstones, nr Hexham, Northumberland
☎ 01434 674711

Off the A69 about 4 miles west of Hexham, the **Railway Inn** is a sociable pub open from 12 every day. Jennings ales, hearty home cooking, quiz and bingo nights.

41 THE BAY HORSE HOTEL

59 Upper Town, Wolsingham, Weardale,
Co Durham DL13 3EX
☎ 01388 527220
⊕ www.thebayhorsehotel.com

Wolsingham is one of the oldest market towns in County Durham, and the **Bay Horse Hotel** has long been one of its most distinguished buildings. Owner Richard Chwieseni (Chick) has invested a great deal of time and money in revitalising this fine old hotel, and July 2005 saw the completion of the refurbishment of the seven guest bedrooms, a programme that included the installation of new bathroom suites. Four rooms at the front have balconies that afford

splendid views down the village and across to open countryside. Richard has the services of first-class managers in Trevor and Liz, who provide a warm, relaxing ambience in which visitors and guests feel immediately at ease.

The public areas boast many distinctive, often unique features, including superb old French and Dutch furniture in the bars and restaurant and the clever use of natural branches and twigs as dividing screens between tables. One part of the dining area has a flagstone floor, a wood-burning stove and branches on the ceiling illuminated by pretty little fairy lights. Bar snacks are served at lunchtime, and in the restaurant à la carte and set menus provide a mouthwatering choice of wide appeal. Traditionalists can tuck into fish & chips, sausages & mash or steak & kidney pudding, while the more adventurous might go for ham hock & foie gras terrine, goat's cheese & red pepper parfait, monkfish and mussels in a shallot, celery and Chablis cream or corn-fed chicken breast with roasted garlic, chorizo, saffron and dry sherry.

The hotel's location at the head of Weardale makes it an excellent choice for a relaxing break in a lovely part of the world. The nearby Tunstall Reservoir is a splendid place for walking, picnicking or fishing, and one of the top attractions in the region is the Weardale Railway, a steam railway running between Wolsingham and Eastgate within the North Pennines Area of Outstanding Natural Beauty.

42 SIMONBURN TEA ROOMS AND B&B

Simonburn, nr Hexham, Northumberland
☎ 01434 681321

Ann Maddison brings a wealth of experience in the licensed trade to **Simonburn Tea Rooms and B&B**. In an attractive village half a mile from the Hexham-Bellingham road, the property has three roles. In the Tea Rooms, visitors can relax and enjoy a selection of home-prepared hot and cold dishes and snacks, and three comfortable bedrooms cater for guests staying awhile in this pleasant part of the world. The handsome stone house, which has a lovely garden, also serves as the village shop and Post Office.

43 THE HADRIAN HOTEL

Front Street, Wall, Hexham NE46 4EE
☎ 01424 681232 Fax: 01424 681512
e-mail: lindsay13@btinternet
🌐 www.hadrian.hotel.com

The Hadrian Hotel is housed in a charming, ivy-clad, stone building, sat on the roadside in the tiny village of Wall. Dating from the 1700s, it is seen locally as the gateway to Hadrian's Wall and the Northumberland National Park. Its cosy interior is elegantly furnished with heavily draped sash windows, richly

upholstered furniture, bare brick fireplaces and tasteful antiques and ornaments. A varied menu ranging from game pie and hearty steaks to simple snacks is served in the restaurant.

44 THE ROYAL HOTEL

Priestpopple, Hexham,
Northumberland NE46 1PQ
☎ 01434 602270 Fax: 01434 604084
e-mail: service@hexham-royal-hotel.co.uk
🌐 www.hexham-royal-hotel.co.uk

Priestpopple is the charmingly named main street of Hexham, and the **Royal Hotel** with its unique golden dome has been a distinctive landmark since 1820. Recent refurbishment has enhanced the already considerable appeal of the hotel, where the accommodation comprises ten bedrooms ranging from singles to a family room. Mr Ants Bar is a lively spot for enjoying a fine range of draught and continental beers, wines, spirits and cocktails, and Sammy Joanna's hosts regular live entertainment. The tariff is based on B&B, but the hotel owns the excellent Dalchini Indian restaurant next door.

45 THE COUNTY HOTEL

Priestpopple, Hexham,
Northumberland NE46 1PS
☎ 01434 603601
🌐 www.thecountyhexham.co.uk

Peter Harding, a leading light in the field of Northumberland tourism, runs the **County Hotel**, a fine Victorian building on the quaintly named main street of Hexham. Beyond the classic revolving door entrance, Peter and his family welcome guests in the smart, comfortable public areas, which include a choice of eating options in the restaurant and bistro. There's plenty to explore in Hexham and the surrounding countryside, and with its seven en suite bedrooms the County Hotel is an ideal base.

111

46 THE SUN INN

Main Street, Acomb, nr Hexham,
Northumberland NE46 4PW
☎ 01434 602934

A cheerful ambience and excellent home cooking have helped to make the **Sun Inn** a great favourite among the residents of Acomb and nearby towns and villages. Visitors to Acomb will also be charmed by the pleasant, relaxed surroundings, and four

cosy bedrooms (two en suite) provide an ideal base for tourists. The inn's printed menu and daily specials provide

plenty of choice for diners, and among the favourites are lasagne, cottage pie, steaks and a mixed grill that's guaranteed to satisfy the biggest appetite. Pub hours are from 5 o'clock Monday to Friday and from noon on Saturday and Sunday.

47 THE ROSE & CROWN

Slaley, nr Hexham,
Northumberland NE47 0AA
☎ 01434 673263
🖥 www.theroseandcrown.co.uk

Dating from the mid-19th century, the **Rose & Crown** is a classic village pub with a strong following among local residents and visitors to the area. Hosts Stephen and Siobhan Hughes are both talented cooks, and together

with their chef they have really put the inn on the map as a place for a meal. Bar and restaurant menus make excellent use of prime fresh

ingredients, and regular customers include visitors from the nearby Slaley Hall Golf & Country Club. The Rose & Crown also caters for guests staying overnight in three upstairs en suite bedrooms with televisions and beverage trays.

48 DYVELS HOTEL

Station Road, Corbridge, nr Hexham,
Northumberland NE45 5AY
☎ 01434 633633
e-mail: dyvels.corbridge@virgin.net

Helen Murray is the owner, hostess and cook at **Dyvels Hotel**, a fine stone building with attractive gardens. The long bar is a pleasant spot for enjoying a chat and a glass of Black Sheep or one of the guest ales at any time of day, but it's the quality of the cooking that has really put this place on the map. On Monday Helen earns her day out of the kitchen, but on the other six days of the

week her hearty home cooked dishes such as a terrific steak & ale pie have a strong and loyal local following.

The market town of Corbridge, once the capital of the ancient Kingdom of Northumbria, is well worth taking time to explore, with a fine Saxon church, Roman relics and walks along the Tyne among the attractions. The Dyvel's five en suite guest bedrooms provide every comfort, and it's best to book well ahead, as the rooms are understandably always in demand at this very pleasant, civilised place.

49 THE GOLDEN LION

Hill Street, Corbridge,
Northumberland NE45 5AA
☎ 01434 632216
e-mail: lindel@peel166.freeserve.co.uk
🌐 www.vizual4u.co.uk/goldenlion

On a prominent corner site in Corbridge, the **Golden Lion** has an open-plan interior with plenty of space for visitors to enjoy the Peel family's genuinely warm hospitality. Wholesome, hearty pub food is served every lunchtime and Monday to Thursday evenings, and six well-appointed en suite bedrooms make the pub an ideal base for discovering the rich history of the area. The building is a case of recycling par excellence, the stones coming from a nearby country mansion that itself used stones from disused Roman bath houses.

50 BARRASFORD ARMS HOTEL

Barrasford, nr Hexham,
Northumberland NE48 4AA
☎ 01434 681237 Fax: 01434 681237
e-mail: barrasfordarms@fsnet.co.uk
🌐 www.barrasfordarms.com

The Milburn family provide guests at the **Barrasford Arms Hotel** with a choice of accommodation to suit all pockets and requirements. Close to Hadrians Wall and several Roman forts, it is an ideal base for walkers and tourists in a region rich in scenic and historic attractions.

The hotel has a selection of double and single rooms, all with en suite facilities, while the Holiday Cottage provides self-catering accommodation in two twin rooms and a double. The third option is the Camping Barns, an ideal base camp for outdoor activity holidays. Each of the two units sleeps up to 8 guests.

51 THE RAILWAY HOTEL

Church Street, Haydon Bridge,
Northumberland NE47 6JG
☎ 01434 684254

The Railway Hotel is a family-run pub in the centre of Haydon Bridge, with a strong following both of local residents and of visitors to a region rich in history. On a prominent corner site on the A69, the 18th century inn has been tastefully refurbished by Michael and Susan Zellas, who have invested a lot of time and effort in the improvements. Food is an important part of the business, and in the bar and dining area home-cooked meals can be enjoyed with a glass or two of wine or beer. The coffee shop caters for lighter appetites. The guest accommodation comprises three excellent rooms.

52 HADRIANS LODGE HOTEL

Hindshield Moss, North Road, Haydon
Bridge, Northumberland NE47 6NF
☎ 01434 684867 Fax: 01434 684867
e-mail: hadrianslodge@hadrianswall.co.uk
🌐 www.hadrianswall.co.uk

Hadrians Lodge Hotel caters for walkers, tourists, anglers and lovers of nature and fresh air with comfortable en suite rooms and a well-stocked bar.

53 OLD REPEATER STATION

Military Road, Grindon, nr Haydon Bridge,
Northumberland NE47 6NQ
☎ 01434 688668
e-mail: les.Gibson@tiscali.co.uk
🌐 www.hadrians-wall-bedandbreakfast.co.uk

The Old Repeater Station is an eco-friendly stone building with a choice of bunk beds or en suite twins. Snacks and meals available.

54 THE GOLDEN LION

Market Square, Allendale, nr Hexham,
Northumberland NE47 9BB
☎ 01434 683225

Michael and Margaret Stonehouse are
carrying out a major programme of
refurbishment, both inside and out, at the
Golden Lion, where they have an equally
warm welcome for familiar faces and first-
time
visitors.
The
superb
home-
cooked
food is a
big
attraction,
with
highlights
including superb steaks form the local farmer,
and the home-made ice cream rounds things
off in style. Improvements include
refurbishing the three guest bedrooms, which
are due to come on stream for the summer
of 2006.

56 THE MILECASTLE INN

North Road, Cawfields, nr Haltwhistle,
Northumberland NE49 9NN
☎ 01434 321372
e-mail: clarehind@aol.com
⊕ www.milecastle-inn.co.uk

Kevin Hind behind the bar and Clare in the
kitchen keep the locals and visitors to this
historic region happy at the **Milecastle Inn**. It
stands on a corner site just north of
Haltwhistle, and
behind the sturdy
stone exterior the
bar and snug are in
keeping with the
inn's 17th century
origins. Attached to
the snug is a
pleasant restaurant
serving a fine variety of classic pub dishes,
including super pies and casseroles and fresh
salads. Two real ales are kept on pump, and the
pub also has a good selection of wines and malt
whiskies. Among the attractions nearby are
Hadrian's Wall, the Roman Army Museum and
the milecastle that gives the pub its name.

55 ALLENDALE TEA ROOMS

Market Place, Allendale, nr Hexham,
Northumberland NE47 9BD
☎ 01434 683575
e-mail: allendaletearooms@btinternet.com
⊕ www.allendale-tearooms.co.uk

On the market place of a town exactly
halfway between the Sussex coast and the
northern tip of Scotland, **Allendale Tea
Rooms** serve traditional home-cooked food
in a friendly, relaxed atmosphere. The choice
runs from breakfast to light lunches, Sunday
roasts, main meals and a tempting selection
of cakes and pastries. Popular with both

locals and passing
trade, the tea rooms
are open from 10-5
Tuesday to
Saturday, 11-5
Sunday, also
Mondays on Bank
Holidays and in
high season. Above
the tea rooms are
two well-kept
rooms for B&B.

HIDDEN PLACES GUIDES

Explore Britain and Ireland with
Hidden Places guides - a fascinating
series of national and local travel
guides.

Packed with easy to read information
on hundreds of places of interest as
well as places to stay, eat and drink.

Available from both high street and
internet booksellers

For more information on the full range
of *Hidden Places* guides and other
titles published by Travel Publishing
visit our website on

www.travelpublishing.co.uk
or ask for our leaflet by phoning
0118-981-7777 or emailing
info@travelpublishing.co.uk

57 THE OTTERBURN TOWER HOTEL

Otterburn, Northumberland NE19 1NS
☎ 01830 520620 Fax: 01830 521504
🌐 www.otterburntower.com

The **Otterburn Tower Hotel** is an imposing fortified building set in 32 acres of beautiful gardens and woodland in the midst of the Northumberland National Park. The original building on this site was founded by a cousin of William the Conqueror as a bastion against the marauding Scots, and history has touched the place on many occasions down the centuries. In 1388 it resisted an attack by the Scots after the bloody Battle of Otterburn. Its most famous owner was 'Mad' Jack Hall, who was executed at Tyburn for high treason.

Peace descended long ago at this splendid place, whose historic beauty is seen in every room with original features such as beams, panelling and stone floors in the public areas. These are every bit as imposing as the handsome façade would suggest: the hall with its huge open fireplace and oak panelling, the morning room, the elegant little bar, the drawing room with its remarkable Florentine marble fireplace.

The 18 en-suite bedrooms, each individual in style, combine a respect for the age and pedigree of the house with all the expected modern comforts; top of the range is a fine four-poster bridal suite. Food is taken very seriously at Otterburn Tower, and the head chef and his team seek out the very best produce – including beef and lamb from the owners' farm – to create superb dishes with a worldwide inspiration. The nearby River Rede is a source of excellent trout and salmon, and herbs and salads come from the hotel's own kitchen garden. The grounds are one of the hotel's greatest assets, and the terraced lawns provide an ideal setting for anything from afternoon tea or a pre-dinner drink to a wedding reception or any other special occasion. A variety of outdoor pursuits, including fishing, shooting, golf and birdwatching, can be arranged by the staff, and the area around the hotel is perfect for walking, cycling and discovering the rich variety of historic and scenic attractions.

58 ELM TREE COFFEE SHOP

**High Street, Rothbury,
Northumberland NE65 7TE
☎ 01669 621337**

Helen Renton and her family have built up a fine reputation for quality and value for money in their ten years at the **Elm Tree Coffee Shop**. In this Victorian town house looking down the main street from its elevated site, two rooms create a delightful, unfussy ambience in which to enjoy good honest home cooking. Counter service provides excellent teas, coffees and hot and

cold drinks to accompany scones, cakes, filled rolls, toasted sandwiches, jacket potatoes and daily specials.

The Renton family and their staff are notably friendly, willing and helpful, ensuring that every visit here is a real pleasure. The Elm Tree is open from 10 o'clock to 5 (to 4 off season) seven days a week. The town of Rothbury needs plenty of time to explore, and one of the many attractions close to the Elm Tree is the National Trust's Cragside, a fine mock-Tudor Victorian mansion that was once the home of the industrialist Sir William Armstrong.

59 THE TURKS HEAD

**High Street, Rothbury,
Northumberland NE65 7TC
☎ 01669 620434**

In a prime location on the main street of Rothbury, the **Turks Head** is a family-friendly hostelry with a traditional bar, a cosy restaurant, B&B rooms and a pleasant beer garden. Cask ales head the list of drinks available throughout the day, and excellent home-cooked dishes (including super meat pies) are served

every lunchtime except Saturday and also Friday and Saturday evenings. With its two comfortable en suite bedrooms, the inn is a fine base for discovering the delights of Rothbury, for a walking holiday or for exploring the valley of the River Coquet.

60 RYECROFT HOTEL

**Wooler, Northumberland NE71 6AB
☎ 01668 281459 Fax: 01668 282214
e-mail: ryecrofthtl@aol.com
⊕ www.ryecroft-hotel.com**

The Corbett family welcome visitors to the **Ryecroft Hotel**. Nine en suite rooms provide a great base for a holiday. Good home cooked food and Real Ale.

61 THE COLLINGWOOD ARMS

**Main Street, Cornhill-on-Tweed,
Northumberland TD12 4UH
☎ 01890 882424 Fax: 01890 883644
enquiries@thecollingwoodarmshotel.co.uk
⊕ www.thecollingwoodarmshotel.co.uk**

Traditional hospitality, good food and comfortable guest bedrooms bring visitors to the **Collingwood Arms** in a village close to the Scottish Borders.

62 THE ANGLERS ARMS

Weldon Bridge, Longframlington,
Northumberland NE65 8AX
☎ 01665 570271 Fax: 01665 570041
e-mail: johnyoung@anglersarms.fsnet.co.uk
🌐 www.anglersarms.com

Starting life in the mid-18th century as a coaching inn, the **Anglers Arms** is now a very popular and comfortable pub, restaurant and hotel. Owner John Young, his management and staff have all played their part in building the enviable reputation the place enjoys and its well-earned accolade as 'a legend in the very heart of Northumberland'.

Antiques, bric a brac, hand-painted wall tiles and fishing memorabilia assist in creating a really appealing ambience, and the restaurant is located in a beautifully restored Pullman carriage from British Railway days. This is the atmospheric setting for enjoying English cooking at its very best, highlighted by an abundance of fresh fish and shellfish, local beef and lamb and mouthwatering desserts. The eight en suite bedrooms, which combine period charm with up-to-date amenities, provide a splendid base for a walking or touring holiday or for fishing on a free-to-residents stretch of the River Coquet.

63 EMBLETON HALL

Longframlington, nr Morpeth,
Northumberland NE65 8DT
☎ 01665 570249 Fax: 01665 570056
🌐 www.embletonhall.com

Embleton Hall is a fine manor house set serenely in five acres of lovely landscaped gardens. Trevor and Judy Thorne, lovers of country life and all things rural, run this refined yet very relaxed country house hotel, where the 13 individually appointed guest bedrooms run from singles to a four-poster room and a family suite.

The cooking is as excellent as every other aspect of the Hall, and the choice includes both bar meals and a table d'hôte menu of fine modern dishes. Among the many amenities are a croquet lawn and grass tennis court.

64 THE NEW INN

Longframlington, nr Morpeth,
Northumberland NE65 8AD
☎ 01665 570268 Fax: 01665 570872

Set in great walking country, with a wealth of scenic and historic attractions, the **New Inn** is a recently refurbished 19th century coaching inn. The inn is gaining a growing reputation as a fine place for a meal, and the daily changing menu tempts with pub classics such as sausages & mash, chilli, filled Yorkshire puddings and steak pie. In the same ownership is the nearby Fram Park (Tel: 01665 570502) offering self-catering accommodation in Finnish-designed log cabins.

65 BLACK BULL

Etal Village, Cornhill on Tweed,
Northumberland TD12 4TL ☎ 01890 820200
e-mail: karenwitchyp@aol.com
🌐 www.blackbulletal.com

An adorable white washed, thatched roofed pub, straight off a picture postcard, the **Black Bull** dates from the late 13th century. Set back from the road, behind a few picnic benches where customers can enjoy a pint al fresco and admire the overflowing hanging baskets in summer. Inside the pub is as charming and rustic as it is on the outside. Food is mostly home made and is simply, honest Northumbria cooking using local produce and fresh fish.

66 THE FOX & HOUNDS

Main Street, Wylam,
Northumberland NE41 8DL
☎ 01661 853246

The **Fox & Hounds** is a popular, well-kept village pub serving good food six days a week (no food Monday).

67 THE JIGGERY POKERY

65 Square, Stocksfield, Northumberland
NE43 7BY
☎ 01661 842256

The **Jiggery Pokery** combines a busy tea room with a shop crammed with all sorts of collectables and bric-a-brac.

68 THE RISING SUN

Banktop, Crawcrook, Tyne & Wear
☎ 0191 413 3316 Fax: 0191 413 4339

On a hill above the River Tyne, the **Rising Sun** is a lively, friendly pub run since the early 1980s by Pauline Baxter and Brian Keating. Built in the 17th century and much extended down the years, the pub is a very pleasant place for a drink or a meal. A wide choice of beers, wines, spirits and soft drinks is served in the elegant Tulip Bar, and in the

striking conservatory-style restaurant the regularly changing menu proposes a fine choice of dishes.

The chef sets great store by fresh seasonal ingredients, and the talents of him and his team have made this one of the most popular eating places in the area. The printed menu is supplemented by daily specials such as lemon & cracked pepper mackerel, Goan chicken curry, beef stew with dumplings and roasted butternut squash strudel. Open all day, every day, the Rising Sun stands above the main street of Crawcrook, close to the A695 and a few miles west of Newcastle-upon-Tyne.

69 THE ANGLERS ARMS

Sheepwash Bank, Choppington, nr Morpeth,
Northumberland NE62 5NB
☎ 01670 822300
e-mail:
theanglersarmssheepwash@btinternet.com

The **Anglers Arms**
is a convivial family-
run pub east of
Morpeth, serving
drinks and snacks,
and with five en suite
B&B rooms.

70 THE FLEECE INN

Bondgate Without, Alnwick,
Northumberland NE66 1PR
☎ 01665 603036

Visitors to the family-
run **Fleece Inn** can
look forward to a
traditional ambience,
locally brewed ales and
honest home cooking –
the mince with
dumplings is a winner!

71 NARROWGATE RESTAURANT

Narrowgate, Alnwick,
Northumberland NE66 1JG
☎ 01665 602050

Alnwick is a place of many attractions, and
after a walk round this fascinating town the
Narrowgate Restaurant is ready to cater for
visitors'
thirsts and
appetites. In
the daytime
this 300-
year-old
building is a
busy family
coffee shop
serving a
selection of
hot and cold
snacks and
meals (and
traditional

Sunday lunch), while on Thursday to Sunday
evenings it becomes an intimate à la carte
restaurant with a tempting menu that includes
excellent steaks.

72 THE ODDFELLOWS ARMS

**Narrowgate, Alnwick,
Northumberland NE66 1JN
☎ 01665 605363**

Julie and Andrew Little, who took over at the beginning of 2005, welcome all-comers to the **Oddfellows Arms,** which stands in the old part of town close to the Castle used as Hogwarts School in the *Harry Potter* films – the Castle walls are opposite the front door. The pub's interior is stylish and inviting, and when the sun shines the spacious beer garden/patio is a very pleasant alternative.

Regularly changing guest ales are served in the bar, and in the restaurant a good choice of bistro-style dishes to suit all tastes is served every lunchtime and evening. Alnwick is a place well worth taking time to explore, with the abbey remains, St Michael's Church, a museum and parks among the attractions apart from the magnificent Castle, and the Oddfellows Arms is an ideal base for tourists. The three guest bedrooms all have en suite facilities, television and beverage tray.

73 THE WIDDRINGTON INN

Widdrington, nr Morpeth,
Northumberland NE61 5DY
☎ 01670 760260 Fax: 01670 760166

North of Morpeth on the road up to Amble and beyond, the 100-year-old **Widdrington Inn** is in the excellent care of Billy Shaw and Julia Watson. They have built up a great relationship with the locals, who come here for the convivial ambience and for the impressive selection of home-cooked snacks and meals. Oak features strongly in the bar's furniture and fittings, and when the sun shines the picnic tables in the garden come into their own.

74 THE MASONS ARMS

Rennington, nr Alnwick,
Northumberland NE66 3RX
☎ 01665 577275 Fax: 01665 577894
e-mail: bookings@masonsarms.net
⊕ www.masonsarms.net

In the heart of England's Border Country, the **Masons Arms** is a fine inn and restaurant a short drive from the A1. A former coaching inn dating back some 200 years, it has been comfortably modernised for today's guests while retaining much of its original charm. Local  ales quench thirsts in the bar, and home-cooked dishes are served in the bar and in the dining rooms. The guest accommodation is divided between the main building, the courtyard stable block and an Executive annexe; all the rooms are tastefully furnished and decorated, centrally heated and very well appointed.

75 THE PACK HORSE

Ellingham, Chathill,
Northumberland NE67 5HA
☎ 01665 589292
e-mail: thepackhorseinn@hotmail.com
⊕ www.thepackhorseinn.org.uk

The area around Ellingham has many places of interest, and after a busy time sightseeing, the bar, lounge and dining room of the **Pack Horse** beckon the thirsty and hungry visitor. This fine old inn at one end of the village has been a popular meeting place for nearly 200 years, and Maureen Scott, her family and staff are continuing the tradition of hospitality in

fine style. Locals and visitors relax over a drink in the cheerful surroundings of the bar, which boasts a feature fireplace and an impressive collection of china jugs and mugs.

The food choice caters for all tastes and appetites with a daily changing selection that runs from baguettes, salads and jacket potatoes to cod in beer batter, liver & bacon, fish and meat pies, curries, the day's roast and vegetarian dishes. The Pack Horse also has five superior guest bedrooms with en suite facilities, television, drinks tray and clock-radio. A full English breakfast starts the day. An alternative to this accommodation is an adjoining cottage let on a weekly basis.

76 THE SCHOONER

78 North Street, Seahouses,
Northumberland NE68 7SB
☎ 01665 720455

The **Schooner** is an 18th century stone building which offers fine hospitality and smart, spacious B&B rooms.

77 BONARSTEADS

Northumberland Road, Berwick-upon-Tweed, Northumberland TD15 2AS
☎ 01289 302906
e-mail:
viviannelaurathompson@btinternet.com

Bonarsteads, with its warm, friendly ambience is a hub of the local community serving drinks and meals lunchtime and evenings.

78 DOOLALLY

52 Bridge Street, Berwick-upon-Tweed,
Northumberland TD15 1AQ
☎ 01289 306796
e-mail: kim.Kirkby@virgin.net

Kim Kirkby was for many years an executive chef in her home city of York before moving north and transferring her talents to **Doolally**. In this delightful café-bistro in the older part of Berwick visitors look forward to first-class cooking in warm, relaxed surroundings, and Kim has quickly established Doolally as one of the top eating places in the area.

Preparation and presentation both win high praise on a daytime menu that includes ciabattas and baked potatoes with interesting fillings, scones and cakes, accompanied by excellent teas and coffees, hot chocolate or cold drinks. On Fridays and Saturdays, a regularly changing evening menu tempts with such dishes as baked sea bass with lemon and oregano, rack of lamb with a raspberry jus, and pasta with roast vegetables and three cheeses. A blackboard lists the evening's selection of wines and beers.

79 APPLE INN

Lucker, nr Belford,
Northumberland NE70 7JH
☎ 01668 213450
e-mail: appleinnlucker@aol.com

Bob behind the bar and Jayne in the kitchen make a great team at the **Apple Inn**, where the owner the Duke of Northumberland drops in for a drink from time to time. The spotless interior is rich in traditional charm, a perfect spot for enjoying a chat over a glass of Belhaven Best. In the 30-cover restaurant, the menu provides a good variety of home-cooked dishes. Close Monday until 6 o'clock.

80 THE WHITE SWAN

Lowick, nr Berwick-upon-Tweed,
Northumberland TD15 2UD
☎ 01289 388249
e-mail: thewhiteswan@onetel.net.uk
🌐 www.bcbiz.co.uk/whiteswan

In a charming little village just four miles from the A1, the **White Swan** retains all the traditional appeal of its 18th century origins. Christine and Phil Raine have a real treat in store for hungry visitors, as the menu of home-cooked dishes served

in the lovely restaurant provides an impressive choice that includes some 30 main courses! For guests staying awhile the inn has two fresh, bright rooms, both generously sized, with modern en suite facilities.

81 THE ROB ROY RESTAURANT WITH ROOMS

Dock Road, Tweedmouth,
Northumberland TD15 2BE
☎ 01289 306428 Fax: 01289 303629
e-mail: therobroy@ic24.net
🌐 www.therobroy@ic24.net

The **Rob Roy** is a public house with an award-winning restaurant using local produce. Also five en suite bedrooms.

Accommodation in Northumbria

The accommodation featured in this section includes hotels, inns, guest houses, bed & breakfasts and self catered establishments. Each establishment has an entry number which is used to identify its location on the map below and its name and short address in the list below the map. The entry number can also be used to find more information and contact details for the accommodation in the ensuing pages. In addition full details of all this accommodation may be found on the Travel Publishing website - www.travelpublishing.co.uk. This website has a comprehensive database of accommodation covering the whole of Britain and Ireland.

ACCOMMODATION

82	The Garden House, Durham
83	Ash House, Cornforth
84	The Bay Horse Inn, Brandon Village
85	Altonlea Lodge, Seaton Carew
86	The George, Darlington
87	The Bridge House, Piercebridge
88	Dromonby Hall Farm, Kirkby-in-Cleveland
89	Zetland Hotel, Marske-by-the-Sea
90	The Crown & Crossed Swords, Shotley Bridge
91	Penny's Tea Rooms, Barnard Castle
92	Cronniwell Village Inn, Hamsterley
93	The Bowes Incline Hotel, Birtley
94	High Force Hotel, Forest-in-Teesdale
95	Hauxwell Grange Cottages, Marwood
96	The Rose & Crown, Mickleton
97	Teesdale Hotel, Middleton-in-Teesdale
98	The Strathmore Arms, Holwick
99	Edge Knoll Farm Cottages, Hamsterley
100	The Cross Keys Inn, Eastgate
101	Burnside Cottages, Edmundbyers
102	The Bay Horse Hotel, Wolsingham
103	The Rookhope Inn, Rookhope
104	Rose Hill Farm, Eastgate
105	Simonburn Tea Rooms and B&B, Simonburn
106	Thistlerigg Farm, High Warden
107	The Hadrian Hotel, Wall
108	The Royal Hotel, Priestpopple
109	The County Hotel, Priestpopple
110	The Sun Inn, Acomb
111	The Rose & Crown, Slaley
112	The Hermitage, Swinburne

113	Dyvels Hotel, Corbridge
114	The Hayes, Corbridge
115	The Golden Lion, Corbridge
116	Crookhill Farm, Newton
117	Barrasford Arms Hotel, Barrasford
118	Ovington House, Ovington
119	The Railway Hotel, Haydon Bridge
120	Hadrians Lodge Hotel, Haydon Bridge
121	Old Repeater Station, Grindon
122	The Otterburn Tower Hotel, Otterburn
123	Allendale Tea Rooms, Allendale
124	Beeswing Lodge, Elsdon
125	Ryecroft Hotel, Wooler
126	The Turks Head, Rothbury
127	The Anglers Arms, Weldon Bridge
128	Embleton Hall, Longframlington
129	The New Inn, Longframlington
130	The Collingwood Arms, Cornhill-on-Tweed
131	The Anglers Arms, Choppington
132	The Masons Arms, Rennington
133	The Oddfellows Arms, Narrowgate
134	The Pack Horse, Ellingham
135	The Schooner, Seahouses
136	Rowena, Seahouses
137	Whyteside House, Berwick-upon-Tweed
138	The Retreat & 40 Ravensdowne, Berwick-upon-Tweed
139	Roxburgh Guest House, Spittall
140	Tweed View, East Ord
141	The White Swan, Lowick
142	The Rob Roy Restaurant with Rooms, Tweedmouth

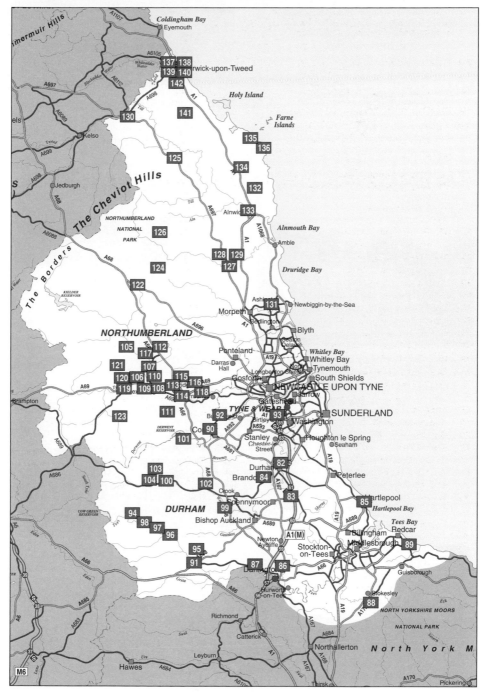

82 THE GARDEN HOUSE

North Road, Durham DH1 4NQ
☎ 0191 384 3460
e-mail: gardenhousedurham@aol.com

Paul Mash brought a wealth of experience in the licensed trade when he took over the **Garden House** with his family at the beginning of 2005. Close to the city centre and an easy walk to the Cathedral, this attractively modernised coaching house serves a good selection of beers and lagers, bar snacks, and a full menu in the conservatory restaurant. The Garden House also has five smart en suite bedrooms for guests spending time exploring Durham's many places of interest.

83 ASH HOUSE

24 The Green, Cornforth, nr Durham,
Co Durham DL17 9JH
☎ 01740 654654
e-mail: delden@btinternet.com

Opposite the large green in a village five miles south of Durham, **Ash House** is a beautifully appointed early Victorian country house combining antique furnishings and period charm with up-to-date comfort. The guest bedrooms, which include two splendid four-poster rooms, are elegant and spacious,  and all are equipped with washbasins, television, hospitality tray, clock radio and hairdryer. One of the very best B&Bs in the region, Ash House is a perfect spot to unwind and an ideal base for tourists.

84 THE BAY HORSE INN

Brandon Village, nr Durham DH7 8ST
☎ 0191 378 0498

Clair and Peter are the new owners of the **Bay Horse Inn**, an attractive hostelry on a corner site near the A690 southwest of Durham City. It's a fine base for exploring the sights of Durham and the surrounding area, and the 10 modern en suite guest rooms include a family room sleeping up to four.

The rooms are in a single-storey building at the back of the hotel, with disabled access and parking right outside. Clair and Peter have the services of a talented chef who gets his meat from a top local butcher and other supplies from the best local sources. The restaurant is open for lunch and dinner every day, and the accomplished cooking is matched by very good service and excellent value for money.

85 ALTONLEA LODGE

19 The Green, Seaton Carew,
Hartlepool TS25 1AT
☎ 01429 271289
e-mail: bookings@altonlea.co.uk
🌐 www.altonlea.co.uk

Close to the seafront at Seaton Carew,
Altonlea Lodge is a family-run guest house
with a particularly warm and welcoming feel.
The bedrooms – singles, doubles, twins and a
family

room – are
shared
between
the late-
18th
century
main house
and a
newly built
annexe,

and most enjoy views of the sea or the pretty
garden. Owner Olwen Bryan makes sure
that guests start the day with an excellent
breakfast. Secure parking is available at the
rear of the property.

86 THE GEORGE

Bondgate, Darlington DL3 7LB
☎ 01325 481686

David Nicholls woos the locals with a fine
selection of real ales and good unpretentious
food at the **George**, where he has been the
host since 1998. Sandwiched among shops in
the town
centre, it has
been a
Darlington
landmark since
1837, and
remains a
popular, no-
nonsense all-
day venue for a
drink. Food is
served from
11 to 3
Monday to
Saturday. The
George also
has four well-
priced rooms
for B&B.

87 THE BRIDGE HOUSE

Piercebridge, nr Darlington,
Co Durham DL2 3SG
☎ 01325 374727

In a lovely setting, with a garden running
down to the River Tees, **The Bridge House**
offers comfortable
guest
accommodation in
three spacious
rooms. Excellent
breakfast; packed
lunch available.

88 DROMONBY HALL FARM

Busby Lane, Kirkby-in-Cleveland, Stokesley,
N Yorkshire TS9 7AP ☎ 01642 712312
e-mail: pat@dromonby.co.uk
🌐 www.dromonby.co.uk

Guests will enjoy the scenic setting, smart
modern accommodation and the super
breakfasts at
**Dromonby Hall
Farm** given a rating
of 3 Diamonds by
Visit Britain.

89 ZETLAND HOTEL

9 High Street, Marske-by-the-Sea,
Tees Valley TS11 6JQ
☎ 01642 483973
e-mail: annallsopp@btconnect.co.uk

Ann Allsopp has a friendly greeting for
everyone at the **Zetland Hotel**, which stands
in the centre of Marske-by-the-Sea, just down
the coast from Redcar. Open every day from
11, this handsome 19th century hotel has
public and lounge bars and a pretty restaurant
serving generous portions of unpretentious
dishes. The coast and countryside have plenty
to offer, and the Zetland provides a very
pleasant base with six comfortable bedrooms.

90 THE CROWN & CROSSED SWORDS

**Shotley Bridge, nr Consett,
Co Durham DH8 0HU
☎ 01207 502006**

Shotley Bridge is the place where steel-making started in this region. It became a spa town, and its prosperity has a legacy in many fine houses that survive. One of them, originally a swordmaking warehouse, is now the **Crown & Crossed Swords**, near the A68 and a short distance for Consett. Run by the same family for 50 years, the pub has a delightful traditional bar, an upstairs restaurant and 10 good-sized bedrooms for B&B guests.

91 PENNY'S TEA ROOMS

**Market Place, Barnard Castle, Co Durham
☎ 01833 637634**

Penny's has recently added overnight accommodation to its established role as a popular all-day tea room and licensed restaurant. Traditional home-made food. Open Tue-Sat 9-5, Sun 10-5, also Bank Holidays.

Explore Britain and Ireland with *Hidden Places* guides - a fascinating series of national and local travel guides.

www.travelpublishing.co.uk

0118-981-7777

info@travelpublishing.co.uk

92 CRONNIWELL VILLAGE INN

**Victoria Terrace, Hamsterley,
nr Newcastle NE17 7SH
☎ 01207 561992 Fax: 01207 560719**

Keith and Lynda Telford have recently taken over the **Cronniwell Village Inn** from Lynda's mother, so the family connection remains strong. Always a favourite with the locals, the inn also attracts a considerable passing trade, as it stands on the A694 road that links Consett with Newcastle-upon-Tyne.

The inn has had several incarnations in its life, and the pretty village pub of today has been tastefully modernised while retaining a delightful traditional appeal, and prints and pictures in the public rooms depict the area in former days. Keith and Lynda started to serve food in July 2005, and a free supper accompanies the Sunday night quiz. The inn also provides a convenient base for motorists, whether on business or leisure travel, and there are plans to add to the 5 bedrooms currently available.

93 THE BOWES INCLINE HOTEL

Northside, Birtley, Co Durham DH3 1RF
☎ 0191 410 4756
🌐 www.bowesinclinehotel.co.uk

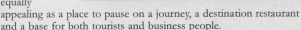

The **Bowes Incline** is a hotel, pub and restaurant in a beautiful setting with magnificent views across the rolling countryside. It lies just off the A1 within a

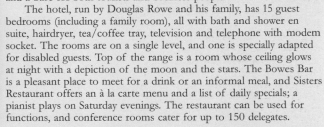

short walk of the amazing Angel of the North, and is equally

appealing as a place to pause on a journey, a destination restaurant and a base for both tourists and business people.

The hotel, run by Douglas Rowe and his family, has 15 guest bedrooms (including a family room), all with bath and shower en suite, hairdryer, tea/coffee tray, television and telephone with modem socket. The rooms are on a single level, and one is specially adapted for disabled guests. Top of the range is a room whose ceiling glows at night with a depiction of the moon and the stars. The Bowes Bar is a pleasant place to meet for a drink or an informal meal, and Sisters Restaurant offers an à la carte menu and a list of daily specials; a pianist plays on Saturday evenings. The restaurant can be used for functions, and conference rooms cater for up to 150 delegates.

94 HIGH FORCE HOTEL

Forest-in-Teesdale, nr Barnard Castle,
Co Durham DL12 0XH
☎ 01833 622222
e-mail: mickclegg@btinternet.com
🌐 www.highforcehotel.com

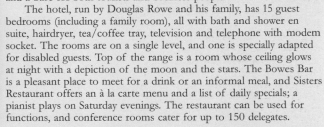

Michael and Vicky Clegg have been at the helm of the famous **High Force Hotel** since 2003, and the improvements they have made in all areas have enhanced its reputation as one of the finest in the region. It was originally a hunting lodge, with royalty among its patrons, and photographs in the bar recall a visit by the future King Edward VII. The day rooms have a very comfortable,

traditional appeal, and the immaculate bedrooms, all with full en suite facilities, guarantee a peaceful night's sleep.

The day starts with an excellent breakfast, and every lunchtime and evening Vicky and her team prepare a fine selection of bar and restaurant meals. Mick's speciality is their own recipe and award winning High Force cask ales, Cauldron Snout and Forest XB. Just minutes from the hotel there are wonderful walks along the banks of the Tees, but the main local attraction is the one that gives the hotel its name – the spectacular waterfall that is one of the wonders of the English landscape.

95 HAUXWELL GRANGE COTTAGES

Marwood, nr Barnard Castle,
Co Durham DL12 8QU
☎ 01833 695022 Fax: 01833 695022
e-mail: hauxwellvmp@supaworld.com
🌐 www.hauxwellgrangecottages.co.uk

Set in the scenic countryside two miles north of Barnard Castle, **Hauxwell Grange Cottages** are equipped with everything needed for a relaxing self-catering break. Curlew Cottage (sleeps 2) and Stone Byre (sleeps 4) are both warm, well furnished and comprehensively fitted. They have a 4 star rating and have wonderful views and a private terrace. Children are welcome, and for a larger group of family or friends the cottages can be hired together. Resident owners Val and Rob

Pearson welcome guests with a basket of wine, tea, coffee, sugar, biscuits and milk.

96 THE ROSE & CROWN

Mickleton, nr Middleton-in-Teesdale,
Co Durham
☎ 01833 640381

The **Rose & Crown** is a handsome greystone building standing on the B6281 between Romaldkirk and Middleton-in-Teesdale. It's a great base for a sporting, walking or touring holiday, and the three guest bedrooms all have washbasins, television and tea/coffee tray. At the back of the pub is a large caravan park looking out over open countryside. The Rose & Crown is popular with locals and motorists, with pleasant bars and a dining area serving rotating real ales and traditional English dishes.

97 TEESDALE HOTEL

Market Square, Middleton-in-Teesdale, nr
Barnard Castle, Co Durham DL12 0QG
☎ 01833 640264
e-mail: john@falconer0.wanadoo.co.uk
🌐 www.teesdalehotel.com

Guests return year after year to the **Teesdale Hotel**, which started life as a coaching house in the 17th century. Hospitality is in generous supply here, and the lounge bar is a warm, comfortable and convivial place where guests and non-residents are equally welcome, and residents also have their own lounge for relaxing after the day's activities or planning the next day's trips. The 14 well-appointed bedrooms include singles, twins, doubles and a family room, and all have en suite facilities.

The hotel also offers a wide choice of bar and restaurant meals and is also a pleasant spot for morning coffee or afternoon tea. Middleton-in-Teesdale, the capital of Upper Teesdale, enjoys a superb setting, in the market place surrounded by green hills. It is an ideal centre for a walking holiday or for exploring both Teesdale and the entire North Pennines; among the many nearby attractions are High Force, England's largest waterfall, Cauldron Snout, England's largest cascade, other dramatic falls and several historic castles.

98 THE STRATHMORE ARMS

Holwick, nr Middleton-in-Teesdale,
Co Durham DL12 0NJ
☎ 01833 640362
⊕ www.strathmore20atbtbusiness.co.uk

The **Strathmore Arms** is a traditional
country pub in a superb setting close to the
River Tees. Coal fires blaze a welcome in the
classic bar and dining area, where real ales
and hearty home-cooked food keep visitors
happy (connoisseurs of real ale head here for

the beer
festivals
held three
times a
year). With
4 en suite
bedrooms,
the inn is a
perfect
base for a

walking holiday: the Pennine Way runs
close by, and a wealth of scenic attractions
includes the spectacular High Force
waterfall. Adjacent to the inn is a campsite
with toilet and washing facilities.

99 EDGE KNOLL FARM COTTAGES

Hamsterley, nr Bishops Auckland,
Co Durham ☎ 01388 488537
e-mail: vacationfarm@hotmail.com

In a lovely country setting, **Edge Knoll
Farm Cottages** is
the perfect base for a
walking or touring
holiday, with a
variety of outdoor
activities available.

100 THE CROSS KEYS INN

Eastgate, nr Stanhope, Weardale,
Co Durham
☎ 01388 517234

Tourists, walkers and cyclists join the locals at
the **Cross Keys
Inn**, where the
new tenants
provide a warm,
genuine welcome.
Home-cooked
food, 2 B&B
rooms.

101 BURNSIDE COTTAGES

The Burnside, Edmundbyers,
Co Durham DH8 9NY
☎ 01207 255257

Brenda Brown has lived here for 25 years,
and in a converted stable block next to her
home she offers top-quality self-catering
accommodation in **Burnside Cottages**. Four
state-of-the-art units are built, furnished and
fitted to the highest standards, with all mod
cons provided in Kingfisher and Robin (1
bedroom in each) and Woodpecker and Owl
(2 bedrooms).

The lovely country setting makes this a perfect base
for walkers, birdwatchers and lovers of the open air,
and the cottages are only a short drive form the A68,
with easy access north to Hadrian's Wall, the
Northumberland National Park and Scotland, and
Bishop Auckland, Darlington and points south in the
other direction. Bookings are usually by the week, but
Brenda will do split weeks and B&B if the cottages are
otherwise free. No smoking

102 THE BAY HORSE HOTEL

59 Upper Town, Wolsingham, Weardale,
Co Durham DL13 3EX
☎ 01388 527220
🌐 www.thebayhorsehotel.com

Wolsingham is one of the oldest market towns in County Durham, and the **Bay Horse Hotel** has long been one of its most distinguished buildings. Owner Richard Chwieseni (Chick) has invested a great deal of time and money in revitalising this fine old hotel, and July 2005 saw the completion of the refurbishment of the seven guest bedrooms, a programme that included the installation of new bathroom suites. Four rooms at the front have balconies that afford

splendid views down the village and across to open countryside. Richard has the services of first-class managers in Trevor and Liz, who provide a warm, relaxing ambience in which visitors and guests feel immediately at ease.

The public areas boast many distinctive, often unique features, including superb old French and Dutch furniture in the bars and restaurant and the clever use of natural branches and twigs as dividing screens between tables. One part of the dining area has a flagstone floor, a wood-burning stove and branches on the ceiling illuminated by pretty little fairy lights. Bar snacks are served at lunchtime, and in the restaurant à la carte and set menus provide a mouthwatering choice of wide appeal. Traditionalists can tuck into fish & chips, sausages & mash or steak & kidney pudding, while the more adventurous might go for ham hock & foie gras terrine, goat's cheese & red pepper parfait, monkfish and mussels in a shallot, celery and Chablis cream or corn-fed chicken breast with roasted garlic, chorizo, saffron and dry sherry.

The hotel's location at the head of Weardale makes it an excellent choice for a relaxing break in a lovely part of the world. The nearby Tunstall Reservoir is a splendid place for walking, picnicking or fishing, and one of the top attractions in the region is the Weardale Railway, a steam railway running between Wolsingham and Eastgate within the North Pennines Area of Outstanding Natural Beauty.

103 THE ROOKHOPE INN

Rookhope, Weardale,
Co Durham DL13 2BD
☎ 01388 517215 Fax: 01388 517861
e-mail: chris@rookhope.com
⊕ www.rookhope.com

Chris Jones has made a fine job of restoring the **Rookhope Inn** to its status as both a convivial village local and a place to seek out for food and accommodation. Real ales from Jennings Cockermouth Brewery and a fine selection of wines and malts are served in the bar, and classic

English dishes offer excellent value for money; freshly cut sandwiches provide a lighter alternative at lunchtime. Very much the hub of village life, the inn has a games room and regularly hosts live music evenings. For overnight guests there are five well-appointed bedrooms. Dogs are very welcome.

104 ROSE HILL FARM

Eastgate, nr Stanhope, Weardale,
Co Durham DL13 2LB
☎ 01388 517209 Fax: 01388 517209
e-mail: info@rosehillfarmbb.co.uk
⊕ www.rosehillbb.co.uk

On the A689 Bishop Auckland-Alston road, **Rose Hill Farm** stands in an area of great natural beauty, with interesting walks in the wooded valley or on the wild moors. The five well-appointed bedrooms are shared between

the main house and the former dairy; two of them are suitable for families, and another room sports a

jacuzzi. A superb farmhouse breakfast gets the day under way, and in the evening anything from a light snack to a 3-course meal is offered, with some dishes featuring home-reared beef and lamb. Packed lunches can be supplied for guests exploring the area. Fishing is available nearby.

105 SIMONBURN TEA ROOMS AND B&B

Simonburn, nr Hexham, Northumberland
☎ 01434 681321

Ann Maddison brings a wealth of experience in the licensed trade to **Simonburn Tea Rooms and B&B**. In an attractive village half a mile from the Hexham-Bellingham road, the property has three roles. In the Tea Rooms, visitors can relax and enjoy a selection of home-prepared hot and cold dishes and snacks, and three comfortable bedrooms cater for guests staying awhile in this pleasant part of the world. The handsome stone house, which has a lovely garden, also serves as the village shop and Post Office.

106 THISTLERIGG FARM

High Warden, nr Hexham,
Northumberland NE46 4SR
☎ 01434 602041 Fax: 01434 602041

The warmth of the welcome is in keeping with the cosy ambience of **Thistlerigg Farm**, a working farm with three rooms for B&B and great views. Open April-October.

Looking for:

- *Places to Visit?*
- *Places to Stay?*
- *Places to Eat & Drink?*
- *Places to Shop?*

www.travelpublishing.co.uk

107 THE HADRIAN HOTEL

Front Street, Wall, Hexham NE46 4EE
☎ 01424 681232 Fax: 01424 681512
e-mail: lindsay13@btinternet
🌐 www.hadrian.hotel.com

The Hadrian Hotel is housed in a charming, ivy-clad, stone building, sat on the roadside in the tiny village of Wall. Dating from the 1700s, it is seen locally as the gateway to Hadrian's Wall and the Northumberland National Park. Its cosy interior is elegantly furnished with heavily draped sash windows, richly

upholstered furniture, bare brick fireplaces and tasteful antiques and ornaments. A varied menu ranging from game pie and hearty steaks to simple snacks is served in the restaurant.

108 THE ROYAL HOTEL

Priestpopple, Hexham,
Northumberland NE46 1PQ
☎ 01434 602270 Fax: 01434 604084
e-mail: service@hexham-royal-hotel.co.uk
🌐 www.hexham-royal-hotel.co.uk

Priestpopple is the charmingly named main street of Hexham, and the **Royal Hotel** with its unique golden dome has been a distinctive landmark since 1820. Recent refurbishment has enhanced the already considerable appeal of the hotel, where the accommodation comprises ten bedrooms ranging from singles to a family room. Mr Ants Bar is a lively spot for enjoying a fine range of draught and continental beers, wines, spirits and cocktails, and Sammy Joanna's hosts regular live entertainment. The tariff is based on B&B, but the hotel owns the excellent Dalchini Indian restaurant next door.

109 THE COUNTY HOTEL

Priestpopple, Hexham,
Northumberland NE46 1PS
☎ 01434 603601
🌐 www.thecountyhexham.co.uk

Peter Harding, a leading light in the field of Northumberland tourism, runs the **County Hotel**, a fine Victorian building on the quaintly named main street of Hexham. Beyond the classic revolving door entrance, Peter and his family welcome guests in the smart, comfortable

public areas, which include a choice of eating options in the restaurant and bistro. There's plenty to explore in Hexham and the surrounding countryside, and with its seven en suite bedrooms the County Hotel is an ideal base.

110 THE SUN INN

Main Street, Acomb, nr Hexham,
Northumberland NE46 4PW
☎ 01434 602934

A cheerful ambience and excellent home cooking have helped to make the **Sun Inn** a great favourite among the residents of Acomb and nearby towns and villages. Visitors to Acomb will also be charmed by the pleasant, relaxed surroundings, and four cosy bedrooms (two en suite) provide an ideal base for tourists. The inn's printed menu and daily specials provide

plenty of choice for diners, and among the favourites are lasagne, cottage pie, steaks and a mixed grill that's guaranteed to satisfy the biggest appetite. Pub hours are from 5 o'clock Monday to Friday and from noon on Saturday and Sunday.

111 THE ROSE & CROWN

Slaley, nr Hexham,
Northumberland NE47 0AA
☎ 01434 673263
⊕ www.theroseandcrown.co.uk

Dating from the mid-19th century, the **Rose & Crown** is a classic village pub with a strong following among local residents and visitors to the area. Hosts Stephen and Siobhan Hughes are both talented cooks, and together

with their chef they have really put the inn on the map as a place for a meal. Bar and restaurant menus make excellent use of prime fresh ingredients, and regular customers include visitors from the nearby Slaley Hall Golf & Country Club. The Rose & Crown also caters for guests staying overnight in three upstairs en suite bedrooms with televisions and beverage trays.

112 THE HERMITAGE

Swinburne, nr Hexham,
Northumberland NE48 4DG
☎ 01434 681248 Fax: 01434 681110
e-mail: katie.stewart@themeet.co.uk

Three beautifully appointed bedrooms provide accommodation at **The Hermitage**, a superb country mansion with lovely gardens and a tennis court. Open April to October.

113 DYVELS HOTEL

Station Road, Corbridge, nr Hexham,
Northumberland NE45 5AY
☎ 01434 633633
e-mail: dyvels.corbridge@virgin.net

Helen Murray is the owner, hostess and cook at **Dyvels Hotel**, a fine stone building with attractive gardens. The long bar is a pleasant spot for enjoying a chat and a glass of Black Sheep or one of the guest ales at any time of day, but it's the quality of the cooking that has really put this place on the map. On Monday Helen earns her day out of the kitchen, but on the other six days of the

week her hearty home cooked dishes such as a terrific steak & ale pie have a strong and loyal local following.

The market town of Corbridge, once the capital of the ancient Kingdom of Northumbria, is well worth taking time to explore, with a fine Saxon church, Roman relics and walks along the Tyne among the attractions. The Dyvel's five en suite guest bedrooms provide every comfort, and it's best to book well ahead, as the rooms are understandably always in demand at this very pleasant, civilised place.

114 THE HAYES

Newcastle Road, Corbridge,
Northumberland NE45 5LP
☎ 01434 632010 Fax: 01434 633069
e-mail: mjct@mmatthews.fsbusiness.co.uk
🌐 www.hayes-corbridge.co.uk

An easy stroll from the centre of Corbridge,
The Hayes is a substantial country house set
in seven acres of quiet, attractive gardens.
Resident owners Campbell and Monica
Matthews offer a choice of guest
accommodation: four bright, bedrooms – two
with en suite facilities – are let on a B&B
basis, and in a small courtyard the former
stables have been converted into two well-
equipped self-catering units sleeping up to 5
guests.

115 THE GOLDEN LION

Hill Street, Corbridge,
Northumberland NE45 5AA
☎ 01434 632216
e-mail: lindel@peel166.freeserve.co.uk
🌐 www.vizual4u.co.uk/goldenlion

On a prominent corner site in Corbridge, the
Golden Lion has an open-plan interior with
plenty of space for visitors to enjoy the Peel
family's genuinely warm hospitality.
Wholesome, hearty pub food is served every
lunchtime and Monday to Thursday evenings,
and six well-appointed en suite bedrooms
make the pub an ideal base for discovering
the rich history of the area. The building is a
case of recycling par excellence, the stones
coming from
a nearby
country
mansion that
itself used
stones from
disused
Roman bath
houses.

116 CROOKHILL FARM

Newton, nr Stocksfield,
Northumberland NE43 7UX
☎ 01661 843117 Fax: 01661 843117
e-mail: catherineleech@amserve.com

Catherine Leech is a perfectionist, which
certainly shows in the immaculate house
where she has three bedrooms for Bed &
Breakfast guests. Tucked away in rural
Northumberland but only seconds from the
A69,

**Crookhill
Farm**
offers,
peace,
comfort
and lovely
views, and
the day
starts with

the very best of farmhouse breakfasts –
evening meals by arrangement. The
farmhouse is an ideal base for lovers of the
open air and for visiting Hadrian's Wall and
many other nearby places of interest. Walkers
welcome. Stabling available.

117 BARRASFORD ARMS HOTEL

Barrasford, nr Hexham,
Northumberland NE48 4AA
☎ 01434 681237 Fax: 01434 681237
e-mail: barrasfordarms@fsnet.co.uk
🌐 www.barrasfordarms.com

The Milburn family provide guests at the
Barrasford Arms Hotel with a choice of
accommodation to suit all pockets and
requirements. Close to Hadrians Wall and
several Roman
forts, it is an
ideal base for
walkers and
tourists in a
region rich in
scenic and
historic
attractions.

The hotel has a selection of double and
single rooms, all with en suite facilities, while
the Holiday Cottage provides self-catering
accommodation in two twin rooms and a
double. The third option is the Camping
Barns, an ideal base camp for outdoor activity
holidays. Each of the two units sleeps up to 8
guests.

118 OVINGTON HOUSE

Ovington, nr Stockfield,
Northumberland NE42 6DH
☎ 01661 832442 Fax: 01661 832442
e-mail: lynne@ovingtonhouse.co.uk

Lynne Moffitt has devoted an enormous amount of time and energy turning a distinguished 18th century gentleman's residence into a delightful choice for a Bed & Breakfast or self-catering holiday. Just south of the A69 and close to the River Tyne, the **Ovington House** is set in five acres of mature gardens and grounds, and the day rooms and bedrooms are decorated and furnished in a style perfectly in keeping with the age and pedigree of this outstanding property.

Modern comforts include powerful showers in all three bedrooms. Lynne offers an excellent choice for breakfast and can provide a packed lunch for guests spending the day out and about. An alternative to the B&B is a well-appointed self-catering unit comprising a double room and a twin room. With the A69 and A68 both nearby, the house is ideally placed for both leisure and business travellers. Newcastle is a few miles to the east, and among closer places of interest are the romantic ruins of Prudhoe Castle, one of the finest in the region when built by Henry II, and the fortified manor house of Aydon Castle.

119 THE RAILWAY HOTEL

Church Street, Haydon Bridge,
Northumberland NE47 6JG
☎ 01434 684254

The Railway Hotel is a family-run pub in the centre of Haydon Bridge, with a strong following both of local residents and of visitors to a region rich in history. On a prominent corner site on the A69, the 18th century inn has been tastefully refurbished by Michael and Susan Zellas, who have invested a lot of time and effort in the improvements. Food is an important part of the business, and in the bar and dining area home-cooked meals can be enjoyed with a glass or two of wine or beer. The coffee shop caters for lighter appetites. The guest accommodation comprises three excellent rooms.

120 HADRIANS LODGE HOTEL

Hindshield Moss, North Road, Haydon
Bridge, Northumberland NE47 6NF
☎ 01434 684867 Fax: 01434 684867
e-mail: hadrianslodge@hadrianswall.co.uk
🌐 www.hadrianswall.co.uk

Hadrians Lodge Hotel caters for walkers, tourists, anglers and lovers of nature and fresh air with comfortable en suite rooms and a well-stocked bar.

121 OLD REPEATER STATION

Military Road, Grindon, nr Haydon Bridge,
Northumberland NE47 6NQ
☎ 01434 688668
e-mail: les.Gibson@tiscali.co.uk
www.hadrians-wall-bedandbreakfast.co.uk

The Old Repeater Station is an eco-friendly stone building with a choice of bunk beds or en suite twins. Snacks and meals available.

122 THE OTTERBURN TOWER HOTEL

Otterburn, Northumberland NE19 1NS
☎ 01830 520620 Fax: 01830 521504
⊕ www.otterburntower.com

The **Otterburn Tower Hotel** is an imposing fortified building set in 32 acres of beautiful gardens and woodland in the midst of the Northumberland National Park. The original building on this site was founded by a cousin of William the Conqueror as a bastion against the marauding Scots, and history has touched the place on many occasions down the centuries. In 1388 it resisted an attack by the Scots after the bloody Battle of Otterburn. Its most famous owner was 'Mad' Jack Hall, who was executed at Tyburn for high treason.

Peace descended long ago at this splendid place, whose historic beauty is seen in every room with original features such as beams, panelling and stone floors in the public areas. These are every bit as imposing as the handsome façade would suggest: the hall with its huge open fireplace and oak panelling, the morning room, the elegant little bar, the drawing room with its remarkable Florentine marble fireplace.

The 18 en-suite bedrooms, each individual in style, combine a respect for the age and pedigree of the house with all the expected modern comforts; top of the range is a fine four-poster bridal suite. Food is taken very seriously at Otterburn Tower, and the head chef and his team seek out the very best produce – including beef and lamb from the owners' farm – to create superb dishes with a worldwide inspiration. The nearby River Rede is a source of excellent trout and salmon, and herbs and salads come from the hotel's own kitchen garden. The grounds are one of the hotel's greatest assets, and the terraced lawns provide an ideal setting for anything from afternoon tea or a pre-dinner drink to a wedding reception or any other special occasion. A variety of outdoor pursuits, including fishing, shooting, golf and birdwatching, can be arranged by the staff, and the area around the hotel is perfect for walking, cycling and discovering the rich variety of historic and scenic attractions.

123 ALLENDALE TEA ROOMS

Market Place, Allendale, nr Hexham,
Northumberland NE47 9BD
☎ 01434 683575
e-mail: allendaletearooms@btinternet.com
🌐 www.allendale-tearooms.co.uk

On the market place of a town exactly halfway between the Sussex coast and the northern tip of Scotland, **Allendale Tea Rooms** serve traditional home-cooked food in a friendly, relaxed atmosphere. The choice runs from breakfast to light lunches, Sunday roasts, main meals and a tempting selection of cakes and pastries. Popular with both

locals and passing trade, the tea rooms are open from 10-5 Tuesday to Saturday, 11-5 Sunday, also Mondays on Bank Holidays and in high season. Above the tea rooms are two well-kept rooms for B&B.

124 BEESWING LODGE

by Dunns Farm, Elsdon, nr Otterburn,
Northumberland NE19 1AL
☎ 01669 640219
🌐 www.dunnsfarm.ntb.org.uk

In a beautiful and peaceful rural setting, **Beeswing Lodge** is a superb stone-built conversion for self-catering with 2 bedrooms, a bathroom, a lounge/dining room and a kitchen with all mod cons.

125 RYECROFT HOTEL

Wooler, Northumberland NE71 6AB
☎ 01668 281459 Fax: 01668 282214
e-mail: ryecrofthtl@aol.com
🌐 www.ryecroft-hotel.com

The Corbett family welcome visitors to the **Ryecroft Hotel**. Nine en suite rooms provide a great base for a holiday. Good home cooked food and Real Ale.

126 THE TURKS HEAD

High Street, Rothbury,
Northumberland NE65 7TC
☎ 01669 620434

In a prime location on the main street of Rothbury, the **Turks Head** is a family-friendly hostelry with a traditional bar, a cosy restaurant, B&B rooms and a pleasant beer garden. Cask ales head the list of drinks available throughout the day, and excellent home-cooked dishes (including super meat pies) are served

every lunchtime except Saturday and also Friday and Saturday evenings. With its two comfortable en suite bedrooms, the inn is a fine base for discovering the delights of Rothbury, for a walking holiday or for exploring the valley of the River Coquet.

127 THE ANGLERS ARMS

Weldon Bridge, Longframlington,
Northumberland NE65 8AX
☎ 01665 570271 Fax: 01665 570041
e-mail: johnyoung@anglersarms.fsnet.co.uk
🌐 www.anglersarms.com

Starting life in the mid-18th century as a coaching inn, the **Anglers Arms** is now a very popular and comfortable pub, restaurant and hotel. Owner John Young, his management and staff have all played their part in building the enviable reputation the place enjoys and its well-earned accolade as 'a legend in the very heart of Northumberland'.

Antiques, bric a brac, hand-painted wall tiles and fishing memorabilia assist in creating a really appealing ambience, and the restaurant is located in a beautifully restored Pullman carriage from British Railway days. This is the atmospheric setting for enjoying English cooking at its very best, highlighted by an abundance of fresh fish and shellfish, local beef and lamb and mouthwatering desserts. The eight en suite bedrooms, which combine period charm with up-to-date amenities, provide a splendid base for a walking or touring holiday or for fishing on a free-to-residents stretch of the River Coquet.

128 EMBLETON HALL

Longframlington, nr Morpeth,
Northumberland NE65 8DT
☎ 01665 570249 Fax: 01665 570056
🌐 www.embletonhall.com

Embleton Hall is a fine manor house set serenely in five acres of lovely landscaped gardens. Trevor and Judy Thorne, lovers of country life and all things rural, run this refined yet very relaxed country house hotel, where the 13 individually appointed guest bedrooms run from singles to a four-poster room and a family suite.

The cooking is as excellent as every other aspect of the Hall, and the choice includes both bar meals and a table d'hôte menu of fine modern dishes. Among the many amenities are a croquet lawn and grass tennis court.

129 THE NEW INN

Longframlington, nr Morpeth,
Northumberland NE65 8AD
☎ 01665 570268 Fax: 01665 570872

Set in great walking country, with a wealth of scenic and historic attractions, the **New Inn** is a recently refurbished 19th century coaching inn. The inn is gaining a growing reputation as a fine place for a meal, and the daily changing menu tempts with pub classics such as sausages & mash, chilli, filled Yorkshire puddings and steak pie. In the same ownership is the nearby Fram Park (Tel: 01665 570502) offering self-catering accommodation in Finnish-designed log cabins.

130 THE COLLINGWOOD ARMS

Main Street, Cornhill-on-Tweed,
Northumberland TD12 4UH
☎ 01890 882424 Fax: 01890 883644
enquiries@thecollingwoodarmshotel.co.uk
🌐 www.thecollingwoodarmshotel.co.uk

Traditional hospitality, good food and
comfortable guest
bedrooms bring visitors
to the **Collingwood
Arms** in a village close
to the Scottish Borders.

131 THE ANGLERS ARMS

Sheepwash Bank, Choppington, nr Morpeth,
Northumberland NE62 5NB
☎ 01670 822300
e-mail:
theanglersarmssheepwash@btinternet.com

The **Anglers Arms**
is a convivial family-
run pub east of
Morpeth, serving
drinks and snacks,
and with five en suite
B&B rooms.

132 THE MASONS ARMS

Rennington, nr Alnwick,
Northumberland NE66 3RX
☎ 01665 577275 Fax: 01665 577894
e-mail: bookings@masonsarms.net
🌐 www.masonsarms.net

In the heart of England's Border Country,
the **Masons Arms** is a fine inn and restaurant
a short drive from the A1. A former
coaching inn dating back some 200 years,
it has been
comfortably
modernised
for today's
guests while
retaining
much of its
original
charm. Local

ales quench thirsts in the bar, and home-
cooked dishes are served in the bar and in
the dining rooms. The guest
accommodation is divided between the
main building, the courtyard stable block
and an Executive annexe; all the rooms are
tastefully furnished and decorated,
centrally heated and very well appointed.

133 THE ODDFELLOWS ARMS

Narrowgate, Alnwick,
Northumberland NE66 1JN
☎ 01665 605363

Julie and Andrew
Little, who took
over at the
beginning of
2005, welcome
all-comers to the
**Oddfellows
Arms,** which
stands in the old
part of town

close to the Castle used as Hogwarts School in the
Harry Potter films – the Castle walls are opposite the
front door. The pub's interior is stylish and inviting,
and when the sun shines the spacious beer garden/
patio is a very pleasant alternative.

Regularly changing guest ales are served in the
bar, and in the restaurant a good choice of bistro-
style dishes to suit all tastes is served every
lunchtime and evening. Alnwick is a place well
worth taking time to explore, with the abbey
remains, St Michael's Church, a museum and parks
among the attractions apart from the magnificent
Castle, and the Oddfellows Arms is an ideal base for
tourists. The three guest bedrooms all have en suite
facilities, television and beverage tray.

134 THE PACK HORSE

Ellingham, Chathill,
Northumberland NE67 5HA
☎ 01665 589292
e-mail: thepackhorseinn@hotmail.com
🌐 www.thepackhorseinn.org.uk

The area around Ellingham has many places of interest, and after a busy time sightseeing, the bar, lounge and dining room of the **Pack Horse** beckon the thirsty and hungry visitor. This fine old inn at one end of the village has been a popular meeting place for nearly 200 years, and Maureen Scott, her family and staff are continuing the tradition of hospitality in

fine style. Locals and visitors relax over a drink in the cheerful surroundings of the bar, which boasts a feature fireplace and an impressive collection of china jugs and mugs.

The food choice caters for all tastes and appetites with a daily changing selection that runs from baguettes, salads and jacket potatoes to cod in beer batter, liver & bacon, fish and meat pies, curries, the day's roast and vegetarian dishes. The Pack Horse also has five superior guest bedrooms with en suite facilities, television, drinks tray and clock-radio. A full English breakfast starts the day. An alternative to this accommodation is an adjoining cottage let on a weekly basis.

135 THE SCHOONER

78 North Street, Seahouses,
Northumberland NE68 7SB
☎ 01665 720455

The **Schooner** is an 18th century stone building which offers fine hospitality and smart, spacious B&B rooms.

136 ROWENA

99 Main Street, Seahouses,
Northumberland NE68 7TS
☎ 01665 721309

Four bedrooms for B&B and an adjacent self-catering cottage offer a choice for guests at **Rowena**, where Susanna Hodgson has a warm welcome for one and all.

137 WHYTESIDE HOUSE

46 Castlegate, Berwick-upon-Tweed,
Northumberland TD15 1JT
☎ 01289 331019
e-mail: albert.whyte@onetel.net

Albert Whyte greets young and old alike at **Whyteside House**, a late-Victorian greystone building in the top end of town, with a 4 diamond Silver Award. The whole house has recently been refurbished and the three en-suite

bedrooms, complete with colour TV and hospitality tray, guarantee a peaceful, comfortable night's sleep. Albert's superb breakfast choice is definitely worth getting up for! There is also private off-street parking.

138 THE RETREAT & 40 RAVENSDOWNE

51a Low Green, Berwick-upon-Tweed,
Northumberland TD15 1LX
Mob: 07790843879
e-mail: dorothy@the-retreat-berwick.co.uk
www. the-retreat-berwick.co.uk
40 Ravensdowne, Berwick-upon-Tweed,
Northumberland TD15 1DQ
☎ 01289 306992 Fax: 01289 331606
e-mail: dmuckle@ravensdowne.co.uk
www.ravensdowne.co.uk

The Retreat is a delightful holiday home set in a quiet courtyard. The immaculate self-catering accommodation sleeps 5 and comprises of two bedrooms, a bathroom, a cosy lounge and a large, well-equipped kitchen/dining room. It is decorated and furnished to a very high standard and is rated 4 star by ETC. Owner Dorothy Muckle also offers B&B accommodation at **40 Ravensdowne** rated 4 Diamond by ETC with a Silver Award. Both are non-smoking.

141 THE WHITE SWAN

Lowick, nr Berwick-upon-Tweed,
Northumberland TD15 2UD
☎ 01289 388249
e-mail: thewhiteswan@onetel.net.uk
www.bcbiz.co.uk/whiteswan

In a charming little village just four miles from the A1, the **White Swan** retains all the traditional appeal of its 18th century origins. Christine and Phil Raine have a real treat in store for hungry visitors, as the menu of home-cooked dishes served  in the lovely restaurant provides an impressive choice that includes some 30 main courses! For guests staying awhile the inn has two fresh, bright rooms, both generously sized, with modern en suite facilities.

139 ROXBURGH GUEST HOUSE

Main Street, Spittall, nr Berwick-upon-Tweed, Northumberland TD15 1RP
☎ 01289 306266
e-mail: roxburghhotel@aol.com

Situated close to the beach at Spittall, **Roxburgh Guest House** has 5 bright, spacious rooms for Bed & Breakfast guests.

140 TWEED VIEW

Village Green, East Ord, nr Berwick-upon-Tweed, Northumberland TD15 2NS
☎ 01289 332378 Fax: 01289 332378
e-mail: khdobson@aol.com

Eileen Dobson keeps standards high at **Tweed View**, where the three pristine bedrooms are comfortable and bright and the breakfasts really special. No smoking.

142 THE ROB ROY RESTAURANT WITH ROOMS

Dock Road, Tweedmouth, Northumberland TD15 2BE
☎ 01289 306428 Fax: 01289 303629
e-mail: therobroy@ic24.net
www.therobroy@ic24.net

The **Rob Roy** is a public house with an award-winning restaurant using local produce. Also five en suite bedrooms.

Places of Interest in Northumbria

The selection of places of interest featured in this section includes museums, galleries, castles, historic houses, gardens, churches, cathedrals, gardens, country parks and many other places

worth visiting in Cumbria. Each place of interest has an entry number which is used to identify its location on the map below and its name and short address in the list below the map. The entry number can also be used to find more information and contact details for the places of interest in the ensuing pages. In addition full details of places of interest in this section may be found on the Travel Publishing website – www.travelpublishing.co.uk This website has a large database of places of interest covering the whole of Britain and Ireland.

🏛 PLACES OF INTEREST

143 LOCOMOTION: THE NATIONAL RAILWAY MUSEUM

Hackworth Close, Shildon,
County Durham DL4 1PQ
☎ 01388 777999
🌐 www.railcentre.co.uk

County Durham is famous as being the birthplace of the railways, thanks to the famous Stockton to Darlington railway. Timothy Hackworth was, from 1825, the superintendent engineer on the line, and in 1840, realising the huge potential of rail travel, he resigned to develop the famous Soho Engine works at Shildon, and make his own locomotives. It was here that the first trains to run in Russia and Nova Scotia were built, and many ships were powered by marine engines designed and built on the premises.

Now the whole 15 acre complex, plus his house, form the nucleus for **Locomotion: The National Railway Museum,** which gives a fascinating insight into the early days of rail and steam power in England. Timothy was a true son of the North East, having been born at Wylam-on-Tyne in Northumberland in 1786, and dying in 1850 in the house that now forms part of the museum. He was a born engineer, and one of his earliest machines was the famous "Puffing Billy". He later worked for George Stephenson at his works in Newcastle before moving to the Stockton to Darlington Railway.

Thanks to him, Shildon became the first railway town in the world. Now it attracts thousands of tourists each year who want to find out about the transport revolution that took place in the early 1800s. The Soho engine shed dates back to the 1820s, and houses a Hackworth beam engine (which can operate at the press of a button), the locomotive "Braddyll" (standing on the exact spot where it may have been painted 160 years ago), an 1850s coal wagon and an 1860s passenger coach from the Stockton to Darlington railway. Perhaps one of the most interesting exhibits in the museum is a full sized replica of the "Sans Pareil", a locomotive Timothy built for the Rainhill Trials of 1829 on the Liverpool to Manchester railway. There's also a working rail line from the museum's goods shed to the coal drops at Shildon Station. Visitors can sometimes take trips on the line, being pulled by the locomotive "Merlin". Timothy Hackworth's house has period rooms, models, a marvellous audio visual display and some smaller exhibits.

You don't need to be a railway buff to enjoy Locomotion. It has plenty of hands-on and interactive exhibits, and was voted Visitor Attraction of the Year in 1999 by the Northumbria Tourist Board. Opening Times: Wednesday to Sunday from Good Friday until last Sunday in October 10.00-17.00 daily; Admission charge.

145

144 RACY CASTLE

Staindrop, County Durham DL2 3AH
☎ 01833 660202 Fax: 01833 660169
e-mail: admin@rabycastle.com
🌐 www.rabycastle.com

Raby Castle is not merely a medieval fortress but the home of Lord Barnard. Pass through the Castle gates and be captivated by the historic splendour. Built in the 14th century by the Nevills, most of the interior now dates from the 18th and 19th centuries, although its medieval heart remains. Every room, from the grand Entrance Hall to the Servant's Bedroom gives an insight to life throughout the ages.

Picture the arrival of seven hundred knights gathering in the magnificent Baron's Hall and feel the intrigue of the plotting of the Rising of the North in 1569. Today, see the many treasures including the Meissen birds, part of the beautiful porcelain collection. Throughout the Castle, the many rooms display fine furniture and furnishings, impressive paintings and elaborate architecture for all to see. The kitchen, built in 1360, remains almost untouched, showing its original medieval

form. The cooking equipment has been updated and was in use until 1954.

Wander across the terrace in front of the Castle and look out over the lake to the deer park where 200 Red and 200 Fallow deer graze or take time to enjoy a stroll through the historic gardens. See the formal lawns, ornamental pond and rose garden that are bound by grand yew hedges and towering conifer trees. Look back towards the Castle to admire the magnificent view.

Beyond the gardens you will approach the 18th century Coach Houses which now accommodate the fascinating Coach and Carriage Museum. The Raby

State Coach is amongst the finest examples of travel in bygone days. In the Tack Room wonder at the pristine harnesses and trappings. View the original livery worn by the coachman in Edwardian times.

Pause for refreshment and light snacks at the enticing Stable Tea Rooms, where old stalls of the coach horses have been incorporated to create a unique setting. Walk through to the gift shop to buy a present or a memento of your delightful visit to Raby Castle.

145 HARTLEPOOL'S MARITIME EXPERIENCE

Jackson Dock, Maritime Avenue,
Hartlepool TS24 0XZ
☎ 01429 860077 Fax: 01429 867332
e-mail: info@hartlepoolsmaritimeexperience.com
🌐 www.hartlepoolsmaritimeexperience.com

Open every day,
all year round*
and winner of
many tourism
and visitor
attraction

awards, **Hartlepool's Maritime Experience** is a fascinating and enjoyable day out with something to suit all ages. An authentic re-creation of an 18th century seaport which tells the story of life at sea at the time of Captain Cook, Nelson and the Battle of Trafalgar. Featuring authentic reconstructions of period harbour-side shops, children's maritime adventure centre and wooden playship. A film presentation shows how two brothers were press-ganged into serving in the Royal Navy and 'Fighting Ships', an audio/visual tour which allows you to experience the noise and drama of a fierce sea battle. Costumed guides add to your experience and there are regular gun firing, cannon firing and swordfighting displays. Audio tours are available on board HMS Trincomalee, a magnificent ship launched in Bombay in 1817, the last of Nelson's Frigates. She is the oldest floating warship in Britain; restored in Hartlepool and now a major part of this attraction. Explore the Captains Cabin, Mess Deck and Hold. Find out about life at sea in cramped and very difficult conditions. The ship and quayside have been used for many drama and documentary programmes depicting this important time in British history. The Museum of Hartlepool tells the story of the town from prehistoric times to the present day and includes exhibits such as sea monsters, a Celtic 'Roundhouse', the first 'gas illuminated lighthouse', numerous models, computer interactive displays and the paddle steam ship Wingfield Castle with on board coffee shop. *Closed 25th, 26th and 31st December.

146 DARLINGTON RAILWAY CENTRE & MUSEUM

North Road Station, Darlington DL3 6ST
☎ 01325 460532 Fax: 01325 287746
e-mail: museum@darlington.gov.uk
🌐 www.drcm.org.uk

Experience the atmosphere of the steam railway age as you step back in time in the history of North Road

Passenger Station of 1842. See Stephenson's Locomotion No 1 which hauled its first train on the Stockton and Darlington Railway in 1825. Explore the railway heritage of North East England through a collection of engines, carriages and wagons. Open daily 10-5pm, all year except 25th and 26th December and 1st January.

147 BEAMISH MUSEUM

Beamish, County Durham DH9 0RG
☎ 0191 370 4000 Fax: 0191 370 4001
e-mail: museum@beamish.org.uk
🌐 www.beamish.org.uk

No trip to County Durham is complete without a trip to the award-winning **North of England Open Air Museum at Beamish**. Set in 300 acres of countryside, it illustrates life in the North of England in

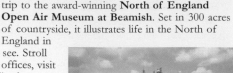

the early 1800s and 1900s. There is so much to see. Stroll down a cobbled street full of shops, banks and offices, visit an old Methodist chapel, find out how life was lived on a farm in the late 19th century, take a trip on a tram or steam train, visit an old dentist's surgery (and be grateful you didn't live in those days, and needed a filling!), walk through a colliery village, and go down a drift mine,

You can also see the world's third oldest surviving railway engine, which dates from 1822, housed in a specially created Great Engine Shed. There's also Pockerley Manor and Horse Yard, based on a small fortified manor house. Here you experience life as it was lived 200 years ago. Stroll the terraced gardens, walk through the fine horse yard, and see the costumes from all these years ago.

Beamish is justly famous as a great day out for all the family. Reasonably priced meals and snacks are available, and there's a friendly shop where you can buy souvenirs.

148 WASHINGTON WILDFOWL & WETLANDS CENTRE

Washington, Tyne and Wear NE38 8LE
☎ 0191 4165454 Fax: 0191 4165801
e-mail: info.washington@wwt.org.uk
🌐 www.wwt.org.uk

WWT Washington is one of nine Centres run by the Wildfowl & Wetlands Trust, a registered charity. Here you can have a fantastic day out seeing, feeding and learning about wetland birds, whilst also helping WWT to conserve wetland habitats and their biodiversity.

At the Heron Hides, closed circuit cameras allow you to see individual nests during the breeding season, of the largest colony of Grey Hreons in the area. A variety of ducks, geese and swans can be seen in the reserve, including the Nene, state bird of Hawaii, saved from the brink of extinction by WWT. Having arrived at Washington in 1986, the Chilean Flamingo colony is now breeding well and often makes use of the Flamingo House, built with a donation from author Catherine Cookson. The James Steel Waterfowl Nursery, built in 1996 is the first

home for most of the ducks and geese that hatch at Washington and special tours take place during the breeding season.

You can take your time to stroll around the nature reserve, or explore Spring Gill Wood with its ponds, streams and woodland. The Hawthorn Wood Wild Bird Feeding Station attracts a variety of woodland birds such as Woodpeckers and Sparrowhawks that can be seen mostly during the winter. The centre also has an adventure play area for children, a waterside café and The Glaxo Wellcome Discovery Centre, with its displays and exhibits.

149 GATESHEAD MILLENIUM BRIDGE

Gateshead, Tyne and Wear
☎ 0191 433 3000 (Gateshead Council)

See one of the world's most stunning riverside landmarks - the **Gateshead Millenium Bridge.** The world's only tilting bridge opens to allow shipping to pass underneath its graceful arches. Don't forget to catch the bridge in the evening, when it is lit by a high-tech light display, able to create dazzling patterns in millions of colours.

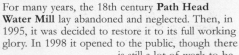

It uses a tilting mechanism to open, turning on pivots on both sides of the river to form a spectacular gateway arch. Two concrete piers hide the massive hydraulic rams, pivots and motors which open the bridge. Each opening or closing takes four minutes, powered by eight electric motors totalling 440 kilowatts or 589 horse power - more power than the fastest sports cars like a Ferrari F50. The main arch rises to 50 metres and is 126 metres wide - but precisely made to a tolerance of 3mm. The weight is over 850 tonnes - enough steel to make 64 double decker buses.

The bridge was designed by Wilkinson Eyre Architects/Gifford & Partners, and built by Gateshead based construction company Harbour & General at a cost of £22 million - almost half of which was paid for by Lottery money through the Millenium Commission.

150 PATH HEAD WATER MILL

Summerhill, Blaydon on Tyne NE21 4SP
☎ 0191 414 6288
e-mail: enquiries@gatesheadmill.co.uk
🌐 www.gatesheadmill.co.uk

For many years, the 18th century **Path Head Water Mill** lay abandoned and neglected. Then, in 1995, it was decided to restore it to its full working glory. In 1998 it opened to the public, though there is still a lot of work to be done. It is located in a picturesque, quiet dell, and here you can see how water was the main source of energy before the advent of the steam engine, and how a mill harnessed the power of water to turn its machinery. A small gallery of photographs shows you the stages in the mill's restoration, plus there's a tearoom. Opening Times: Tuesday-Sunday 11am-3pm in winter and 10am-5pm in summer; Closed Mondays, except for bank holidays; Admission charge.

151 BOWES MUSEUM

Barnard Castle, County
Durham DL12 8NP

☎ 01833 690606 Fax: 01833 637163

e-mail: info@bowesmuseum.org.uk

⊕ www.bowesmuseum.org.uk

The Bowes Museum is one of County Durham's great surprises - a beautiful and grand French château-style museum on the outskirts of the historic town of Barnard Castle. It was built by John Bowes, illegitimate son of the 10th Earl of Strathmore, and his Parisian actress wife, Josephine, Countess of Montalbo, between 1862 and 1875. They wanted to house the vast collection of works of art they had amassed from all corners of Europe so that people from all walks of life could see and enjoy them, but unfortunately they died before their dream was realised.

But realised it eventually was, and today it has an outstanding collection that will take your breath away. County Durham is lucky to have a such a museum and gallery - one that is undoubtedly of international importance. Here the visitor can admire a vast range objets d'arts and paintings, including what is acknowledged to be the most important collection of Spanish paintings in Britain. There are works by Goya and El Greco, and works by painters of the calibre of Canaletto, Boudin and Tiepola can also be found on the walls. Tapestries, ceramics, woodwork, fine furniture and clocks can also be seen - a feast of the finest craftsmanship that could be found in Europe at the time. But John and Josephine Bowes didn't just restrict themselves to the grand and the prestigious. There is also a wonderful display of toys, including the world's first toy train set.

The Museum's most famous exhibit is undoubtedly the Silver Swan. The life-sized bird, with its exquisite silver plumage, is an automaton and musical box, set in a stream made from twisted glass rods with small fish "swimming" among them. When it is wound up, the glass rods rotate, a tinkling tune is played, and the swan preens itself before lowering its head towards the water and seemingly picking up a fish. It then raises its head once more and appears to swallows it.

The museum is under the care of Durham County Council, and runs a regular programme of temporary exhibitions and displays. There are also occasional craft fairs and musical events (programme available from the Museum), plus special free guided tours.The licensed café sells snacks and light meals, and there's a shop where you can buy a souvenir or gift. Parking is free, and, apart from one or two areas, the museum is disabled-friendly. There are also 23 acres of gardens and parkland to enjoy

Opening Times: 11am-5pm daily, except Christmas Day, Boxing Day and New Year's Day

152 ST MARY'S LIGHTHOUSE

St Mary's Island, Whitley Bay NE26 4RS
☎ 0191 200 8650

Just north of Whitley Bay, you'll find **St Mary's Lighthouse** and the adjoining keepers' cottages, situated on a small island which is accessible at low tide. It was built in 1898, and closed in 1984. Now it has been converted into a fascinating small museum and visitor centre by North Tyneside Council. There are 137 steps to the top, though the climb is worth it - the views are  spectacular! If the climb doesn't appeal, you can still see it courtesy of a video at ground level. An exhibition explains the history of the lighthouse and the varied wildlife of the island, which is a nature reserve. There's also a small souvenir shop, and plenty of parking on the mainland. Opening times: Depends on tides; phone for leaflet; Admission charge.

153 THE WEARDALE MUSEUM & HIGH HOUSE CHAPEL

Ireshopeburn, County Durham
☎ 01388 537417
🌐 www.weardalemuseum.co.uk

High House Chapel, built in 1760, is the world's oldest Methodist Chapel still in continuous use. The 'John Wesley's Weardale' exhibition and collection of Methodist memorabilia, have established the Chapel and Museum as a premier Methodist heritage site. The Museum also tells the story of the Westgate Subscription  Library, established in 1788 to promote reading among the working class lead miners. Also here you will see an 1870 Weardale kitchen, furnished as it would have been then, a superb collection of local crystals and fossils, displays of the Weardale Railway and the Victorians shown through photographs and cencus.

154 HIGH FORCE WATERFALL

Middleton-in-Teesdale, County Durham
Enquiries to Raby Estate Office, Middleton-in-Teesdale, County Durham DL12 0QH
☎ 01833 640209 Fax: 01833 640963
e-mail: teesdaleestate@rabycastle.com
🌐 www.rabycastle.com

From its rise as a trickle, high on the heather covered fells at the top of the North Pennines, to the top of the whin sill rock at Forest-in-Teesdale, the River Tees steadily grows and gathers pace. Then it suddenly and spectacularly drops 70 feet. **High Force** is reputed to be the highest unbroken fall of water in  England. You'll feel its awesome power as you begin the approach. There's the peace and quiet of the countryside, but something else - an air of anticipation.

As you begin the descent down the gently sloping, well-maintained path, a muffled rumble reaches your ears. You can enjoy the pretty woodland walk which twists and turns with a different view every few yards, but still the waterfall escapes you. Then the rumble turns into a roar - you can imagine the feel of spray on your face and there's a natural earthy aroma. You peer through the trees and there it is. The sight astounds you. Postcards and photographs can't portray the sheer size of the vertical wall of water - the ceaseless roaring sound - and the almost tangible atmosphere of the place. High Force commands respect. Its power is its beauty, but it must be treated with care. Children should be supervised at all times. High Force is open all year and is spectacular throughout the seasons.

155 KIELDER WATER AND FOREST PARK

Kielder, Northumberland
☎ 01434 220643 (Bellingham Tourist Information Centre)
⊕ www.kielder.org

In a land of astonishing beauty, **Kielder Water and Forest Park** perfectly captures the mood of Northumberland. An inspirational and romantic place where you can escape the trials of everyday life and experience pure tranquility in a truly stunning environment. Kielder, the North Tyne Valley and nearby Wild Redesdale offers a wealth of choice and experiences within an environment where freedom to be tranquil, adventurous or in touch with nature is yours for the taking.

A wide range of recreational opportunities are available, providing something for everyone, whether you are a skilled outdoors enthusiast or looking to absorb the intoxicating sights and sounds at a more sedate pace.

The many activities include walking, cycling, sailing, riding and fishing, and around the park you can find a variety of places to eat and drink, shop, swim or play miniature golf. There is ample parking and several picnic sites.

An 80 seater motor cruiser will take you on a trip around the lake and on board you have use of a bar, shop, lounge and toilets.

156 BELSAY HALL CASTLE AND GARDENS

Belsay, near Ponteland, Northumberland NE20 0DX
☎ 01661 881297 Fax: 01661 881043

Belsay Hall Castle and Gardens is one of the best English Heritage properties in the area. The Grade I listed hall was built for Sir Charles Monck on an estate that already had a castle and Jacobean mansion, and they all stand in 30 acres of beautifully landscaped gardens. There is a magnolia garden, terraces, rhododendrons, a winter garden and croquet lawn, and a quarry garden. In

addition there's free parking, a tearoom (summer only) and various small exhibitions. Opening Times: Daily 24 March -30 September 10am-6pm; 1-31 October 10am-4pm; 1 November-31 March 10am-4pm (except Tue and Wed); closed 24-26 December and 1 January

157 ALNWICK CASTLE

Alnwick, Northumberland NE66 1NQ
☎ 01665 510777
e-mail: enquiries@alnwickcastle.com
🌐 www.alnwickcastle.com

Owned by the Percy family since 1309, **Alnwick** is one of the finest castles in the British Isles. Originally built to defend England's northern border from the Scottish armies, the castle is the family home of the Duke and Duchess of Northumberland. With magnificent views over the River Aln and surrounding countryside, the castle is a few minutes walk from the centre of the historic market town of Alnwick.

Within the massive stone walls, the beautifully kept grounds contain fascinating exhibitions. Discover the history of the Northumberland Fusiliers since 1674 in the Abbot's Tower. Marvel at the richness of Northumberland's archaeological past in the Postern Tower and listen to life as a member of the Percy Tenantry Volunteers (1798-1814) in the Constable's Tower.

At the heart of the castle is the keep. Pass through the medieval towers and enter a wonderful family home. State Rooms, refurbished in the mid 19th century by the Fourth Duke, contain paintings by Canaletto, Van Dyck and Titian. Finely carved wooden panels adorn the walls, windows and ceilings. Children's quiz helps your family learn about Alnwick Castle.

There are various events held throughout the spring and summer, including Birds of Prey displays, horse driving trials and an International Music Festival. Noted as a location for 'Harry Potter', 'Elizabeth' and 'Robin Hood, Prince of Thieves', Alnwick Castle is open daily from 1st April to 31st October.

158 BAMBURGH CASTLE

Bamburgh, Northumberland NE69 7DF
☎ 01668 214515 Fax: 01668 214060
e-mail: bamburghcastle@aol.com
🌐 www.bamburghcastle.com

Standing on a rocky outcrop overlooking miles of beautiful sandy beach, **Bamburgh Castle** dominates the Northumbrian landscape. The castle became the passion of the 1st Baron Armstrong who, in the 1890's, began its renovation and refurbishment. This love of Bamburgh was passed down through the family to the late Lord Armstrong, who personally oversaw the completion of his ancestor's dream.

Today Bamburgh Castle is still the home of the Armstrong family, and visitors are able to enjoy what has been described as the finest castle in all England. The public tour includes the magnificent King's Hall, the Cross Hall, reception rooms, the Bakehouse and Victorian Scullery, as well as the Armoury and Dungeon. Throughout, these rooms contain a wide range of fine china, porcelain and glassware, together with paintings, furniture, tapestries, arms and armour.

The Armstrong Museum, occupying the former Laundry Building, is dedicated to the life and work of the first Lord Armstrong. An inventive engineer, shipbuilder and industrialist, he left a great legacy to the modern age and Tyneside in particular.

The castle is open daily from mid March to the end of October, between 11am and 5pm, and teas and light refreshments are available from The Clock Tower.

Acknowledgement: Copyright Jarrold Publishing, reproduced by kind permission of the publisher.

159 LINDISFARNE PRIORY

Lindisfarne, Northumberland
☎ 01289 389200

Lindisfarne Priory is one of the Holiest Anglo-Saxon sites in England. When you cross the dramatic causeway to Holy Island, you journey into our spiritual heritage. Few places are as beautiful or have such special significance. The corpse of St. Cuthbert was found undecayed in AD 698, and this became one of the most sacred shrines in Christendom. For 1300 years it has been a place of pilgrimage and still is today.

Here you can learn about the Monastery's fantastic wealth and walk in the grounds where brutal Viking raiders plundered the priory, forcing Monks to refuge on the mainland. It is advisable to have a tide table with you when you visit Lindisfarne - at high tide the causeway linking Holy Island to the Northumbrian coast is submerged, cutting the Island off.

There is a sculpture on show entitled "Cuthbert of Farne" which was created by local artist Fenwick Lawson. This sculpture depicts a comtemplative Cuthbert reflecting on his religious life and desire for solitude. His interlaced hands echo the stillness and peace he sought.The Museum features are lively and atmospheric and explain what life was like more than a millenium ago. Open daily except Christmas and New Year, the facilities include parking, toilets, gift shop, souvenir guide and exhibition.

Tourist Information Centres

ADDERSTONE

Adderstone Services
Adderstone Garage
Belford
Northumberland
NE70 7JU
Tel No: 01668 213678
Fax: 01668 213111
e-mail: adderstone@hotmail.com

ALNWICK

2 The Shambles
Alnwick
Northumberland
NE66 1TN
Tel No: 01665 510665 or 01665 605607
Fax: 01665 510447
e-mail: alnwicktic@alnwick.gov.uk

AMBLE

Queen Street Car Park
Amble
Northumberland
NE65 0DQ
Tel No: 01665 712313
Fax: 01665 713838
e-mail: ambletic@alnwick.gov.uk

BARNARD CASTLE

Woodleigh
Flatts Road
Barnard Castle
County Durham
DL12 8AA
Tel No: 01833 690909 or 01833 695320
Fax: 01833 695320
e-mail: tourism@teesdale.gov.uk

BELLINGHAM

Fountain Cottage, Main Street
Bellingham
Near Hexham
Northumberland
NE48 2BQ
Tel No: 01434 220616
Fax: 01434 220643
e-mail: bellinghamtic@btconnect.com

BERWICK-UPON-TWEED

106 Marygate
Berwick upon Tweed
Northumberland
TD15 1BN
Tel No: 01289 330733
Fax: 01289 330448
e-mail: tourism@berwick-upon-tweed.gov.uk

BISHOP AUCKLAND

Town Hall
Market Place
Bishop Auckland
County Durham
DL14 7NP
Tel No: 01388 604922 or 01388 602610
Fax: 01388 604960
e-mail: bishopauckland.touristinfo
@durham.gov.uk

CORBRIDGE

Hill Street
Corbridge
Northumberland
NE45 5AA
Tel No: 01434 632815
Fax: 01434 634269
e-mail: corbridgetic@btconnect.com

CRASTER

Craster Car Park
Craster
Alnwick
Northumberland
NE66 3TW
Tel No: 01665 576007
Fax: 01665 576007
e-mail: crastertic@alnwick.gov.uk

DARLINGTON

13 Horsemarket
Darlington
DL1 5PW
Tel No: 01325 388666 or 01325 388675
Fax: 01325 388667
e-mail: tic@darlington.gov.uk

DURHAM

2 Millennium Place
Durham City
DH1 1WA
Tel No: 0191 384 3720
Fax: 0191 386 3015
0191 301 8533
e-mail: touristinfo@durhamcity.gov.uk

GATESHEAD (CENTRAL LIBRARY)

Central Library
Prince Consort Road
Gateshead
Tyne & Wear
NE8 4LN
Tel No: 0191 433 8420 or 0191 478 2060
text
Fax: 0191 477 7454
e-mail: tic@gateshead.gov.uk

GATESHEAD (VISITOR CENTRE)

Gateshead Visitor Centre
St Mary's Church
Gateshead
NE8 2AU
Tel No: 0191 478 4222 or 0191 477 5380
Fax: 0191 478 7983
e-mail: tourism@gateshead.gov.uk

HALTWHISTLE

Railway Station
Station Road
Haltwhistle
Northumberland
NE49 9HN
Tel No: 01434 322002
Fax: 01434 322470
e-mail: haltwhistletic@btconnect.com

HARTLEPOOL

Hartlepool Art Gallery
Church Square
Hartlepool
TS24 7EQ
Tel No: 01429 869706
Fax: 01429 523408
e-mail: hpooltic@hartlepool.gov.uk

HEXHAM

Wentworth Car Park
Hexham
Northumberland
NE46 1QE
Tel No: 01434 652220
Fax: 01434 652393
e-mail: hexham.tic@tynedale.gov.uk

MIDDLESBROUGH

Middlesbrough Information
    Centre & Box Office
Albert Road
Middlesbrough
TS1 2QQ
Tel No: 01642 729700
Fax: 01642 729935
e-mail: middlesbrough_tic
        @middlesbrough.gov.uk

MIDDLETON-IN-TEESDALE

10 Market Place
Middleton-in-Teesdale
County Durham
DL12 0QG
Tel No: 01833 641001
Fax: 01833 641001
e-mail: middletonplus@compuserve.com

MORPETH

The Chantry
Bridge Street
Morpeth
Northumberland
NE61 1PD
Tel No: 01670 500700
Fax: 01670 500710
e-mail: tourism@castlemorpeth.gov.uk

NEWCASTLE AIRPORT

Tourist Information Desk
Newcastle Airport
Newcastle upon Tyne
Tyne & Wear
NE13 8BZ
Tel No: 0191 214 4422 or 0870 122 1488
Fax: 0191 214 3378 or 0191 214 3363
e-mail: niatic@hotmail.com

NEWCASTLE-UPON-TYNE

Newcastle Information Centre
132 Grainger Street
Newcastle upon Tyne
Tyne & Wear
NE1 5AF
Tel No: 0191 277 8000
Fax: 0191 277 8009 or 0191 277 8010
e-mail: tourist.info@newcastle.gov.uk

NORTH SHIELDS

Unit 18 Royal Quays Outlet Shopping
North Shields
Tyne & Wear
NE29 6DW
Tel No: 0191 200 5895 or 0191 200 8535
Fax: 0191 200 5896 or 0191 200 8703
e-mail: ticns@northtyneside.gov.uk

ONCE BREWED

Northumberland National Park Centre
Military Road, Bardon Mill
Hexham
Northumberland
NE47 7AN
Tel No: 01434 344396
Fax: 01434 344487
e-mail: tic.oncebrewed@nnpa.org.uk

OTTERBURN

Otterburn Mill
Otterburn
Northumberland
NE19 1JT
Tel No: 01830 520093
Fax: 01830 520032
e-mail: tic@otterburnmill.co.uk

PETERLEE

4 Upper Yoden Way
Peterlee
County Durham
SR8 1AX
Tel No: 0191 586 4450
Fax: 0191 518 1786
e-mail: touristinfo@peterlee.gov.uk

ROTHBURY

Northumberland National Park Centre
Church House, Church Street
Rothbury
Northumberland
NE65 7UP
Tel No: 01669 620887
Fax: 01669 620887
e-mail: tic.rothbury@nnpa.org.uk

SEAHOUSES

Seafield Car Park
Seafield Road
Seahouses
Northumberland
NE68 7SW
Tel No: 01665 720884
Fax: 01665 721436
e-mail: seahousesTIC
            @berwick-upon-tweed.gov.uk

SOUTH SHIELDS

South Shields Museum & Gallery
Ocean Road
South Shields
Tyne & Wear
NE33 2HZ
Tel No: 0191 454 6612
Fax: 0191 454 6612
e-mail: museum.tic@s-tyneside-mbc.gov.uk

SOUTH SHIELDS (AMPHITHEATRE)

Sea Road
South Shields
NE33 2LD
Tel No: 0191 455 7411
Fax: 0191 455 7411
e-mail: foreshore.tic@s-tyneside-mbc.gov.uk

STANHOPE

Durham Dales Centre
Castle Gardens
Stanhope
County Durham
DL13 2FJ
Tel No: 01388 527650 or 01388 526393
Fax: 01388 527461
e-mail: durham.dales.centre@durham.gov.uk

STOCKTON-ON-TEES

Stockton Central Library
Church Road
Stockton-on-Tees
TS18 1TU
Tel No: 01642 528130 or 01642 528131
Fax: 01642 675617
e-mail: touristinformation@stockton.gov.uk

SUNDERLAND

50 Fawcett Street
Sunderland
Tyne & Wear
SR1 1RF
Tel No: 0191 553 2000 or 0191 553 2001/2
Fax: 0191 553 2003
e-mail: tourist.info@sunderland.gov.uk

WHITLEY BAY

Park Road
Whitley Bay
Tyne & Wear
NE26 1EJ
Tel No: 0191 200 8535 or 0191 200 5895
Fax: 0191 200 8703 or 0191 200 5896
e-mail: ticwb@northtyneside.gov.uk

WOOLER

Wooler TIC
The Cheviot Centre
12 Padgepool Place
Wooler
Northumberland
NE71 6BL
Tel No: 01668 282123
Fax: 01668 283233
e-mail: woolerTIC
            @berwick-upon-tweed.gov.uk

Towns, Villages and Places of Interest

158

TRAVEL PUBLISHING ORDER FORM

To order any of our publications just fill in the payment details below and complete the order form. For orders of less than 4 copies please add £1 per book for postage and packing. Orders over 4 copies are P & P free.

Please Complete Either:

I enclose a cheque for £ [   ] made payable to *Travel Publishing Ltd*

Or:

Card No: [   ]   Expiry Date: [   ]

Signature: [   ]

Name: [   ]

Address: [   ]

Tel no: [   ]

Please either send, telephone, fax or e-mail your order to:
Travel Publishing Ltd, 7a Apollo House, Calleva Park, Aldermaston, Berkshire RG7 8TN
Tel: **0118 981 7777**   Fax: **0118 982 0077**   e-mail: **info@travelpublishing.co.uk**

	Price	Quantity		Price	Quantity
HIDDEN PLACES REGIONAL TITLES			**COUNTRY PUBS AND INNS**		
Cornwall	£8.99	....	Cornwall	£8.99	....
Devon	£8.99	....	Devon	£8.99	....
Dorset, Hants & Isle of Wight	£8.99	....	Sussex	£8.99	....
East Anglia	£8.99	....	Wales	£8.99	....
Lake District & Cumbria	£8.99	....	**COUNTRY LIVING RURAL GUIDES**		
Northumberland & Durham	£8.99	....	East Anglia	£10.99	....
Peak District	£8.99	....	Heart of England	£10.99	....
Sussex	£8.99	....	Ireland	£11.99	....
Yorkshire	£8.99	....	North East	£10.99	....
HIDDEN PLACES NATIONAL TITLES			North West	£10.99	....
England	£11.99	....	Scotland	£11.99	....
Ireland	£11.99	....	South of England	£10.99	....
Scotland	£11.99	....	South East of England	£10.99	....
Wales	£11.99	....	Wales	£11.99	....
HIDDEN INNS TITLES			West Country	£10.99	....
East Anglia	£7.99	....	**OTHER TITLES**		
Heart of England	£7.99	....	Off the Motorway	£11.99	....
North of England	£7.99	....			
South	£7.99	....			
South East	£7.99	....			
Wales	£7.99	....	**Total Quantity:**	[ ]	
West Country	£7.99	....			
Yorkshire	£7.99	....	**Post & Packing:**	[ ]	
			Total Value:	[ ]	

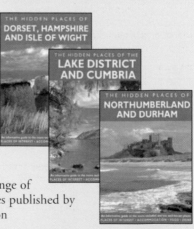

READER REACTION FORM

The *Travel Publishing* research team would like to receive reader's comments on any visitor attractions or places reviewed in the book and also recommendations for suitable entries to be included in the next edition. This will help ensure that the *Hidden Places series of Guides* continues to provide its readers with useful information on the more interesting, unusual or unique features of each attraction or place ensuring that their visit to the local area is an enjoyable and stimulating experience. To provide your comments or recommendations would you please complete the forms below and overleaf as indicated and send to:

**The Research Department, Travel Publishing Ltd,
7a Apollo House, Calleva Park, Aldermaston, Reading, RG7 8TN.**

Your Name:

Your Address:

Your Telephone Number:

Please tick as appropriate:

    Comments ☐   Recommendation ☐

Name of Establishment:

Address:

Telephone Number:

Name of Contact:

READER REACTION FORM

COMMENT OR REASON FOR RECOMMENDATION:

....

....

....

....

....

....

....

....

....

....

....

....

....

....

....

....

....

....

....

....

READER REACTION FORM

The *Travel Publishing* research team would like to receive reader's comments on any visitor attractions or places reviewed in the book and also recommendations for suitable entries to be included in the next edition. This will help ensure that the *Hidden Places series of Guides* continues to provide its readers with useful information on the more interesting, unusual or unique features of each attraction or place ensuring that their visit to the local area is an enjoyable and stimulating experience. To provide your comments or recommendations would you please complete the forms below and overleaf as indicated and send to:

The Research Department, Travel Publishing Ltd,
7a Apollo House, Calleva Park, Aldermaston, Reading, RG7 8TN.

Your Name:

Your Address:

Your Telephone Number:

Please tick as appropriate:

Comments ☐   Recommendation ☐

Name of Establishment:

Address:

Telephone Number:

Name of Contact:

READER REACTION FORM

COMMENT OR REASON FOR RECOMMENDATION:

....

....

....

....

....

....

....

....

....

....

....

....

....

....

....

....

....

....

....

READER REACTION FORM

The *Travel Publishing* research team would like to receive reader's comments on any visitor attractions or places reviewed in the book and also recommendations for suitable entries to be included in the next edition. This will help ensure that the *Hidden Places series of Guides* continues to provide its readers with useful information on the more interesting, unusual or unique features of each attraction or place ensuring that their visit to the local area is an enjoyable and stimulating experience. To provide your comments or recommendations would you please complete the forms below and overleaf as indicated and send to:

**The Research Department, Travel Publishing Ltd,
7a Apollo House, Calleva Park, Aldermaston, Reading, RG7 8TN.**

Your Name:

Your Address:

Your Telephone Number:

Please tick as appropriate:

Comments ☐   Recommendation ☐

Name of Establishment:

Address:

Telephone Number:

Name of Contact:

READER REACTION FORM

COMMENT OR REASON FOR RECOMMENDATION:

....

....

....

....

....

....

....

....

....

....

....

....

....

....

....

....

....

....

READER REACTION FORM

The *Travel Publishing* research team would like to receive reader's comments on any visitor attractions or places reviewed in the book and also recommendations for suitable entries to be included in the next edition. This will help ensure that the *Hidden Places series of Guides* continues to provide its readers with useful information on the more interesting, unusual or unique features of each attraction or place ensuring that their visit to the local area is an enjoyable and stimulating experience. To provide your comments or recommendations would you please complete the forms below and overleaf as indicated and send to:

**The Research Department, Travel Publishing Ltd,
7a Apollo House, Calleva Park, Aldermaston, Reading, RG7 8TN.**

Your Name:

Your Address:

Your Telephone Number:

Please tick as appropriate:

Comments ☐   Recommendation ☐

Name of Establishment:

Address:

Telephone Number:

Name of Contact:

READER REACTION FORM

COMMENT OR REASON FOR RECOMMENDATION:

....

....

....

....

....

....

....

....

....

....

....

....

....

....

....

....

....

....

....

Index of Advertisers

INDEX OF ADVERTISERS

PLACES OF INTEREST

172